ANTHROPOLOGICAL PAPERS

MUSEUM OF ANTHROPOLOGY, UNIVERSITY OF MICHIGAN

NO. 43

PREHISTORIC BIOLOGICAL RELATIONSHIPS IN THE GREAT LAKES REGION

BY

RICHARD GUY WILKINSON

ANN ARBOR

THE UNIVERSITY OF MICHIGAN, 1971

PREFACE

THIS study was begun in the fall of 1964 as a brief description of the skeletal material from the Norton Mounds, a Hopewellian burial mound complex in southwestern Michigan. In the intervening years I have been financially aided by the Museum of Anthropology and the Department of Anthropology of the University of Michigan; this aid is very gratefully acknowledged.

Mr. Charles E. Eyman of the University of Calgary provided me with much of the background necessary for an osteological study such as this, as well as several suggestions on a great variety of problems, for all of which I am most grateful. My thanks also go to Mr. George Stuber of the University of Michigan Museum of Anthropology for his help on the technical aspects of the illustrations in this study.

A special note of thanks goes also to Dr. Georg K. Neumann of Indiana University, and to Mr. Arthur Graves of Saginaw, Michigan. Dr. Neumann permitted me to study the skeletal material from the Pete Klunk Mounds and the Frederick site, and the kind hospitality of Dr. and Mrs. Neumann during my brief stay with them in the summer of 1968 is especially appreciated. Mr. Graves supplied the University of Michigan Museum of Anthropology with the Bussinger site skeletal material. His dedication and the thoroughness of his work should be a model for all non-professional archaeologists.

It is also with sincerest appreciation that I acknowledge the help of professors C. Loring Brace, Stanley M. Garn, James B. Griffin, Ernst Goldschmidt and Frank B. Livingstone, all of whom read this manuscript and provided me with valuable suggestions. Finally, I should like to thank my wife Ellen, to whom fell the onerous task of typing the manuscript.

The author very gratefully acknowledges the financial assistance from the State University of New York for partial payment of the publication costs of this study.

TABLE OF CONTENTS

LIST OF FIGURES

LIST OF PLATES

LIST OF TABLES

INTRODUCTION

THE widespread cultural complex known as Hopewell represents the most intensively studied cultural horizon in eastern North American archaeology. The history of attempts to explain what is now referred to as Hopewellian is long, with serious work dating back to the late eighteenth century. Despite the intensive study, there still remain some questions, the answers to which are important to an understanding of Hopewell on the one hand, and of prehistoric North America on the other. For example, the question of what that "thing" we call Hopewell really is has not been agreed upon. We may thus read of the Hopewellian cult, interaction sphere, culture, phase and so on (see Caldwell, 1964).

Just what Hopewell is, apparently depends upon the emphasis given the various traits which define Hopewell. If, for example, the burial mounds, earthworks and burial offerings are emphasized to the exclusion of or in comparison to the villages and utilitarian artifacts, Hopewell may be seen as a cult (Prufer, 1964*a*). A similar emphasis on exotic materials and environmental location of sites has led to the interaction sphere interpretation (Caldwell, 1964; Struever, 1964). Taking all of these variables into account, considering the time depth involved and viewing Hopewell as an *in situ* development, the Hopewellian populations are best considered a culture or cultural phase (Griffin, 1946, 1958, 1960, 1967).

The question of an indigenous development of Hopewell out of Early Woodland precursors is one which physical anthropology might well help answer. While many archaeologists interpret the evidence as indicative of such an *in situ* development, unanimity is lacking. There is a clear connection between Early Woodland and Hopewellian cultures, primarily on the basis of pottery-making techniques, and the burial mounds which typify Hopewell did not originate with the Hopewellians; some Hopewellian mounds were constructed over existing pre-Hopewellian mounds. Yet there is also evidence for considerable outside contact during the Middle Woodland (Hopewellian) period. Maize makes its first appearance in the Ohio and Illinois areas at this time, the maize most likely coming in from the Southwest. The abundance of exotic raw materials in Hopewellian mounds further attests to the areal extent of Hopewellian contact.

By comparing Hopewellian series to Early Woodland groups from Ohio and Illinois and temporally related skeletal series from the Southwest and Mexico, physical anthropology might be able to clarify the origins of the Hopewellian culture. This approach does have some serious limitations, however. If Hopewellian skeletal remains are scarce, Early Woodland remains are even more so, and the archaeology of Early Woodland cultures in the eastern United States is unknown, relative to the amount of work that has been done on Hopewellian groups.

The Hopewellian culture or complex, as it will be referred to here, arose from Archaic and Early Woodland precursors around 200 B.C. The centers of the Hopewellian culture were located along the Scioto River in southern Ohio and in the Illinois River Valley. Around A.D. 400 the elaborate burial complex disappeared, and was replaced by generalized Late Woodland cultures throughout the eastern United States with the exception of the Deep South, where Ohio Hopewellian influences prevailed.

What is currently known of the Hopewellians is based almost entirely upon artifacts of the material culture, while the people buried in the impressive mounds, surrounded by the equally impressive material objects, have been largely neglected. Cremation, most common in Ohio Hopewell, has undoubtedly caused some of this neglect of the Hopewellians as a biological population, as has the poor condition of many of the uncremated burials. Yet there exists a large number of Hopewellian burials, few of which have been subject to any kind of systematic analysis. One group of 23 adults from the Turner site near Cincinnati has been described (Hooton, 1922), as has one group from Arkansas (Tekiner, 1963), one from Missouri (Stewart, 1943), a small series from the Shultz focus in Kansas (Eyman, 1966; Phenice, 1968) a portion of the burials from the Albany Mounds in northern Illinois (Jamison, 1969) and several other series from Illinois (Neumann, 1937; Neumann and Fowler, 1952; Adis-Castro and Neumann, 1948). In addition, there are Neumann's more general papers, in which he postulates a change in physical type during the Hopewell period. Specifically, the change is from Lenid to Ilinid (Neumann, 1960) or from Otamid to Lenapid (Neumann, 1952*a*). Although the names of the two varieties have changed through time, they are apparently still seen as the same two physical types. A brief paper by Hunter (1968) offers confirmation of Neumann's Lenid to Ilinid shift at the Klunk site in southwestern Illinois, although no evidence in terms of measurements, indices or any other biological information is presented.

What is known of the physical type(s) of the people responsible for the Hopewellian culture is thus presently in the form of a few site reports and generalizations lacking statistical substantiation. Considering this disproportionate amount of knowledge as compared to the wealth of archaeological information, there are several questions which can be asked of the skeletal material, and hopefully the answers can shed light on some of the problems with which the archaeologists are still grappling.

Given the large areal distribution of Illinois Hopewell, what was the nature of this spread? On the basis of shared artifacts, many archaeologists have postulated a direct physical migration, in terms of "Hopewellian conquest (Wray and MacNeish, 1961)," invasion (McGregor, 1958), or by more subtle means, such as population expansion (Struever, 1964). At least part of the Hopewellian spread has been seen as due to stimulus diffusion, trade and/or physical migration (Prufer, 1964*b*).

One area into which a migration is felt by some to have taken place is southwestern Michigan. The Hopewellian sites in southwestern Michigan are definitely linked culturally with Illinois Hopewell, and not the Ohio variant. The absence of sequential steps in Hopewellian development in Michigan, and their presence in Illinois, leads to the conclusion that the Michigan Hopewell resulted from a fairly rapid intrusion of Hopewellian groups from Illinois.

If the Hopewellian expansion into southwestern Michigan was an actual movement of people from Indiana and northern Illinois, selected populations from these areas should exhibit more similarity to each other than that seen between Michigan and Ohio Hopewellian groups on the one hand, and between Michigan Hopewell and Late Woodland groups, on the other. A close biological relationship is only hinted at with our present knowledge, and most of this similarity is in the form of cultural alteration of the skeletal material, in addition to the obvious archaeological similarities. Bifronto-occipital deformation occurs among various Hopewellian groups from Illinois and Ohio (Neumann, 1942). It also occurs among 41 percent of the burials from the Norton Mounds site, the largest Hopewellian complex in Michigan (Flanders, 1965). Post-mortem removal of a plate of bone from the skull also occurs among the Norton crania, with a frequency of 73 percent. Similar plaque removal occurs in one skull from the Utica Mounds (Flanders, 1965), one from the Snyders site and two from the Steuben Mounds (Morse, 1963); all of these sites are located in Illinois. Plaque removal is seen among various

Late Woodland populations from Michigan and Ontario, although of different form, position and technique than that seen in the Norton crania.

Biologically, it is only the presence of ear exostoses among the Norton group which indicated a relationship with Illinois Hopewellian populations prior to this study. The frequencies of occurrence are similar to several of the Illinois populations, and considerably higher than among non-Hopewellian populations. Adis-Castro and Neumann (1948) use the presence of ear exostoses to indicate a different social status of those people buried in the mounds as compared to the cemetery burials, and as indicators of inbreeding within this higher status group.

In addition to the migration problem, it also seems worthwhile to examine the biological relationships between the various Middle Woodland groups and spatially related Late Woodland groups. Such an examination should indicate whether a biological change accompanied the cultural changes that mark the transition from Middle to Late Woodland. Also, the utilization of spatially distant Late Woodland groups should provide information concerning the relationships among these groups. Nearly all of the Late Woodland groups of the Great Lakes region have been assigned to a single variety, Ilinid, by Neumann (1960). How similar are the several Late Woodland series to the Ilinid type-population? Is there sufficient similarity between these groups to warrant the establishment of a variety? Of perhaps more importance, what are the causes of the similarities and differences between the groups?

Neumann (1952*a*:14) defines a variety as "a zoological group of a certain order of differentiation characterized by the possession of a combination of a selected number of inherited morphological attributes. . . . To attain varietal rank the group must be more than a family line or a very local physical type." These varieties were originally established on the basis of presumed migrations from Asia. That such migrations did not occur is well established, but the varieties, according to Neumann (1960), still exist. The existence of at least some of the varieties has been questioned on statistical grounds (Long, 1966), and the results of this study also raise some serious questions concerning the validity of two of Neumann's varieties, Lenid and Ilinid.

Finally, there is the obviously important question concerning the validity of a biological-distance study based, as is this one, on small sample sizes. An attempt has been made to maximize the sample sizes, but even so the samples are unquestionably small. The extent to which the biological relationships arrived at here are valid can be tested on the basis of archaeological information. If two groups which are nearly identical culturally also appear similar in terms of morphology, the assumption can be made that the biometric techniques are in fact producing valid results.

In summary, it is the purpose of this study to examine the biological relationships existing among certain Middle and Late Woodland populations from the Great Lakes area. Specifically, the study concentrates on the problems of Illinois Hopewellian migration into Michigan, certain Middle and Late Woodland population relationships in Illinois and the Great Lakes area, and the apparent causes of these relationships.

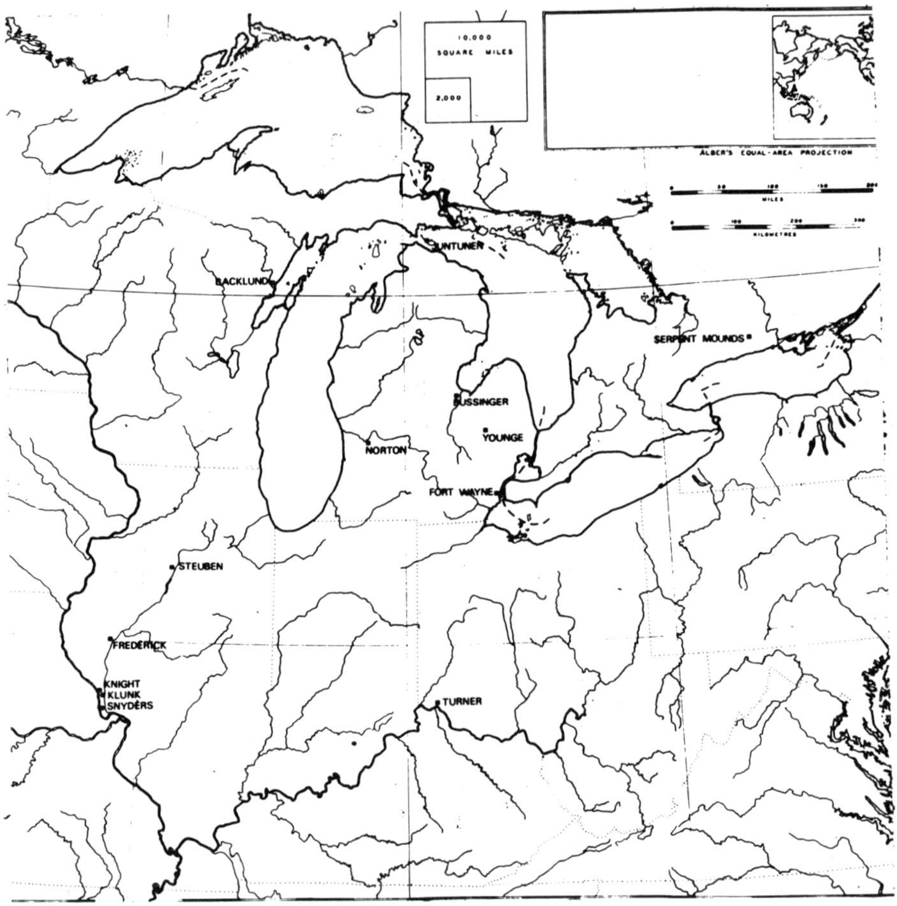

FIG. 1. Location of sites.

I

MATERIALS AND METHODS

MIDDLE AND LATE WOODLAND SITES

SKELETAL material from ten Middle and Late Woodland sites from Michigan and Illinois forms the basis for this study. The sites were chosen on the basis of their possible relevance to the problems set forth earlier, as determined by their geographical position and archaeological information, and on their availability. The Knight and Snyders series are in the United States National Museum, and the Klunk and Frederick series were made available to me by Dr. Georg K. Neumann of Indiana University. All of the series from Michigan and the Steuben site burials from central Illinois are located in the University of Michigan Museum of Anthropology. In this section, the sites from which the material is drawn are briefly described, as is the observational and statistical methodology employed in this study. The locations of the sites discussed here, as well as those used for comparisons, are indicated on the map in Figure 1. The chronological positions of these sites are presented in Table 1.

The terms "Hopewell," "Woodland," "Jersey Bluff" and the subdivisions of Woodland—Early, Middle and Late—are used extensively in this study, and would seem to warrant clarification. The term "Woodland" refers to prehistoric groups in the eastern United States whose culture was characterized by relatively simple grit-tempered pottery and a subsistence level based primarily upon hunting and gathering, although agriculture became increasingly important during the later periods. Woodland populations are further characterized by regional variations in this basic pattern, and are differentiated from the earlier, pre-pottery Archaic groups and the later, strongly agricultural groups of the Mississippi Valley. This generalized Woodland culture is commonly broken down into three divisions; Early, Middle and Late. One can speak of Early, Middle or Late Woodland groups or cultures as there are marked cultural differences between them, but these same terms also carry chronological connotations (Table 1).

TABLE 1

CHRONOLOGICAL AND CULTURAL POSITIONS OF THE GROUPS USED IN THIS STUDY*

		Illinois-Ohio	Michigan-Ontario
1500		HISTORIC TRIBES	
1400			
1300			Juntunen Backlund
1200			
1100	LATE WOODLAND MISSISSIPPIAN		
1000			Younge Bussinger
900			
800		BEGINNING OF INTENSIVE AGRICULTURE	Fort Wayne Mound
700			
600			
500			
400		Knight JERSEY BLUFF HOPEWELL	DECLINE
300			Serpent Mounds
200	MIDDLE WOODLAND	Klunk Frederick Snyders Steuben	
100		Turner	
A.D. 0 B.C.			Norton Mounds
100		HOPEWELL EXPANSION	
200	EARLY WOODLAND	ADENA EARLY HAVANA	
. . . . .			
1000		INITIAL AGRICULTURE	WOODLAND CERAMIC TRADITION

*Adapted from Griffin, 1967:177.

Early Woodland thus refers to populations in the eastern United States known archaeologically from their crude, thick pottery, burial mounds and the beginnings of agriculture. The approximate time span for Early Woodland is from 1000 to 200 B.C.; the term Early Woodland can thus refer to this time period as well. Early Woodland groups are differentiated from the preceding Late Archaic groups primarily by the appearance of pottery.

The Middle Woodland period, from 200 B.C. to about A.D. 400, is characterized by a marked florescence in the burial goods, pottery styles, burial and ceremonial mounds and increasing use of agriculture, including maize cultivation, which were begun in the Early Woodland period. The most elaborate cultural developments during the Middle Woodland period took place in the Scioto Valley, near Chillicothe, Ohio and in the Illinois and Mississippi valleys, these cultures being known as Hopewell. As the Hopewellian sites represent the culmination of the cultural florescence of the Middle Woodland period, "Hopewell" and "Middle Woodland" are often used interchangeably.

Beginning around A.D. 400 there was a marked decrease in the elaborate burial customs and expansive trade networks which characterize Hopewell, and this decline marks the end of the Middle Woodland period and the beginning of the Late Woodland period. As in the previous Early and Middle Woodland periods, Late Woodland was characterized by a number of regional expressions. Agriculture was still practiced, but hunting and gathering were the primary means of subsistence. Indian groups along the eastern coast, in New England and from New York to Minnesota remained typically Late Woodland until the time of European contact, with regional differences.

In the more central area of the eastern United States the post-Hopewellian decline continued as elsewhere. A regional variant of the general Late Woodland cultures, located in west-central Illinois and the adjacent parts of Missouri, shows a transition from Hopewell to Late Woodland, and is known as Jersey Bluff. While the typical Hopewellian extended burials in mounds are common in sites of the Jersey Bluff focus, the pottery style is non-Hopewellian, and the ceremonial grave goods are generally lacking. Most of the mounds from the Knight site, discussed below, are assignable to the Jersey Bluff focus.

Around A.D. 700 there began a second cultural florescence, unrelated to the earlier Hopewellian expansion. The term "Mississippian" is given to those groups which were strongly agricultural, and were located along the Mississippi River and its tributaries from St. Louis, Missouri southward. In time, Mississippian groups expanded northward into Wisconsin, Minnesota and South Dakota, and eastward into Georgia and Ohio.

THE NORTON MOUNDS

The skeletal material from the Norton Mounds was excavated during the summers of 1963 and 1964 by the University of Michigan Museum of Anthropology. The mounds are located in Wyoming Township of Kent County, in southwestern Michigan (see Fig. 1). Six mounds were excavated during the 1963 season (Flanders, 1965), and the largest of the group of mounds, mound M, was excavated the following summer.

Radiocarbon dates have been obtained from decomposed wood and ash from the burial pit of mound H, M-1488 yielding a date of A.D. 160 ± 120, and M-1489 with a date of A.D. 1000 ± 100. The latter date is much too late, and the former would seem to be about 200 years too recent (Flanders, 1965: 293). A third date of 10 B.C. ± 120 (M-1493) was obtained from charcoal in a fire pit at ground level in mound C, the charcoal being in direct association with Naples Stamped rim sherds (Flanders, 1965: 295).

A total of 33 individuals were recovered from 5 of the mounds excavated by the Museum of Anthropology. The sex and age distributions are presented in Table 2. The age distribution, with peaks during childhood and adulthood, reflecting the age groups with the highest mortality, is normal, but the sex distribution shows an abundance of males. The high proportion of males to females is uncommon for Hopewellian mounds, although similar to the proportions found at the Turner site in southern Ohio, where there were 45 males and 19 females (Hooton, 1922:101).

The preservation of the skeletal material ranges from poor to excellent; 8 of the 12 adult males are sufficiently complete to allow metric observations, but the single adult female (I9) is too fragmentary to allow a complete metric description. The metric data (see "Metric Observations," below) from the Norton series is presented in Tables A1, A2 and A3 of the Appendix.

The cultural connections of the Norton Mounds are clearly with Illinois Hopewell, particularly in the northern Illinois Valley (Flanders, 1865:308). Flanders summarizes the position of the Norton Mounds as follows:

> It is clear, however, that the Norton complex represents the earliest large scale Middle Woodland movement into western Michigan from

TABLE 2

SEX AND AGE DISTRIBUTION OF THE NORTON MOUNDS BURIALS

	Sex			Age					
Burial	Male	Female	?	0-5	6-10	11-15	16-25	26-40	40+
H1	X						X		
H2	X								X
H3			X		X				
H4			X	X					
H5			X					X	
Total	2	0	3	1	1	0	1	1	1
J6	X							X	
J7	X								X
J8			X					X	
J-			X		X				
Total	2	0	2	0	1	0	0	2	1
I9		X							X
I10			(2)	(2)					
I11			X		X				
Total	0	1	3	2	1	0	0	0	1
C13	X							X	
C14			X		X				
C15	X						X		
C16	X							X	
C17	X								X
C18			X					X	
Total	4	0	2	0	1	0	1	3	1
M1	X								X
M2	X								X
M3	X								X
M4		X				X			
M5			X	X					
M6	X						X		
M7			X		X				

TABLE 2 (Continued)

	Sex			Age					
Burial	Male	Female	?	0-5	6-10	11-15	16-25	26-40	40+
M8		X					X		
M9			X		X				
M10			X	X					
M11			X	X					
M12			X		X				
M13			X	X					
M14			X	X					
Total	4	2	8	5	3	1	2	0	3
TOTAL	12	3	18	8	7	1	4	6	7

northern Illinois and northwestern Indiana during the first century B.C., a direct physical migration of people who retained strong ties with the Illinois homeland (1965:310).

THE KNIGHT MOUNDS

The Knight mound group consists of 26 mounds located in Hamburg Township, Calhoun County, west-central Illinois. They were first systematically excavated by Dr. Paul F. Titterington and Mr. Walter Wadlo in the 1940's. Dr. Titterington's notes, on file at the University of Michigan Museum of Anthropology, were used by Flanders (1965) in his analysis of the Knight cultural affinities; both sources have been used in the present study.

From the mounds excavated, Titterington reported finding a minimum of 194 individuals; 43 of these are now in the United States National Museum collections. The skeletal material sent to Washington by no means represents a random sample of the available burials, as the Smithsonian collection contains only adults in an excellent state of preservation, or those which bear rather obvious pathologies. Skeletal material not meeting these criteria were either reburied or otherwise disposed of; some were eaten by pigs which wandered into the open burial pit during the night (Flanders, 1965:104).

The non-random representation severely hinders a meaningful demographic analysis of the Knight material, and the situation is further complicated by the fact that the burials do not represent a single temporal population. Most of the Hopewellian burials were removed from the mounds by Mr. Wadlo, and were not preserved. The majority of the burials from the Knight Mounds thus can be assigned to the Jersey Bluff complex. Archaeological evidence indicates that this complex at the Knight site follows the Hopewellian period very closely in time and shows a gradual transition from Late Hopewell into Early Jersey Bluff (J. B. Griffin, personal communication).

The seven extant burials from mound $C^{O}1$ and 19 from $C^{O}2$ are all Jersey Bluff. Mound $C^{O}3$ is represented by four burials, two of which had Canteen vessels in association, and are thus identifiable as Jersey Bluff. A third burial, an extended female (U.S.N.M. 380-107), has no cultural associations, and the fourth, an extended male (U.S.N.M. 380-108), was found with a sheet of mica, an elk metapodial pin, two Norton-variant Snyders points and a cube of galena, all suggesting that this burial, $C^{O}3$-17, is Hopewellian. The two burials remaining from mound $C^{O}4$ (U.S.N.M. 380-110 and -111) are both probably Hopewellian. A final Hopewell burial comes from mound $C^{O}16$, an extended female (U.S.N.M. 380-298) found with antler earspools and exhibiting typical Hopewellian cranial deformation. The other two burials from $C^{O}16$ are Jersey Bluff, as are all three burials from $C^{O}17$ and the six from $C^{O}21$.

The skeletal material available from the Knight Mounds is thus mostly representative of the Early Jersey Bluff complex, with only 4 of the extant 43 burials being Hopewellian. Due to the fact that some burials are represented by post-cranial remains alone, a total of 24 male and 13 female crania are available for study. The metric observations on these individuals are found in Tables B1, B2 and B3 of the Appendix.

Titterington's field notes provide the only source of information on the age and sex distributions of the Knight burials, and the age categories used by Titterington were rather inclusive, with individuals being recorded as adults, adolescents or infants. The sex and age distributions, based on the field notes, are presented in Table 3. As some burials consisted of only scattered long bones, sex and age descriptions were not made, and in other cases the age is not mentioned, hence the discrepancies in the number of individuals in the sex and age categories of Table 3.

TABLE 3

SEX AND AGE DISTRIBUTION OF THE KNIGHT BURIALS

	Sex			Age			
Mound	Male	Female	?	0-10	11-20	21-40	40+
C^{o}1	5	5	10	10	0	7	3
C^{o}2	15	10	5	3	4	15	8
C^{o}3	2	6	5	1	3	7	1
C^{o}4	8	7	4	3	1	15	
C^{o}5	2	2	26	1		8	
C^{o}6			13				
C^{o}7			5				
C^{o}8	1	4	9	5		8	
C^{o}14		1				1	
C^{o}16	6	2	11	5	1	7	2
C^{o}17	4	1	1			2	3
C^{o}21	3	3			2	3	1
C^{o}22	6	5	17	1		17	
Total	52	46	106	29	11	90	18

Bearing in mind the difficulties alluded to above concerning this demographic information, it is at least apparent that the distributions of age and sex do not vary greatly from what we might expect. There are about as many males as females, and the age distribution is normal for pre-industrial populations.

THE PETE KLUNK MOUNDS

The Pete Klunk Mounds are located on a bluff overlooking the Illinois River near Kampsville, Calhoun County, west central Illinois. They were excavated by Gregory H. Perino of the Thomas Gilcrease Foundation, in 1960 and 1961 (Perino, 1968). Archaic, Hopewellian and Jersey Bluff components are all represented at the site.

The skeletal material used in this study from the Klunk Mounds was graciously made available to me by Dr. Georg K.

Neumann, of the Indiana University Department of Anthropology. Since time was a limiting factor in my data gathering, I selected only the most complete skeletons from the collection of around 300 individuals, all of which were removed from the Hopewellian mounds. Such a selective procedure rules out demographic information, but a comprehensive study is to be presented in the near future by Mr. King B. Hunter of Indiana University. I was able to make observations on 21 males and 11 females, all from 5 of the Hopewellian mounds. Mounds 1, 2, 3, 4, 5, 6, 11, 12, and 13 are considered Hopewellian, as is part of mound 7 (Perino, 1968: 14). From mound 1 (11-C°30) observations were made on 8 males and 3 females; of these burials, only one, C°30-57, is identified as being non-Hopewellian (Perino, 1968:37). A radiocarbon date of A.D. 175 ± 75 (M-1161) reaffirms the cultural identification of the other burials (Crane and Griffin, 1963). Observations were made on three males and a female from mound 2 (11-C°31), all of which are Hopewellian.

From mound 5 (11-C°34) I have data on 3 males and 2 females; one of these, C°34-25, may be Late Woodland, as it was a bundle reburial found only 16 inches deep in the mound (Perino, 1968:57), and lacks cranial deformation. Five males and 3 females from mound 7 (11-C°36) were measured, and from mound 11 (11-C°40) I have data on 2 males and 2 females. The metric data and male cranio-facial indices are listed in Tables C1, C2 and C3 of the Appendix.

In comparing my estimates of sex with those recorded by Perino (these latter identifications presumably were made by Hunter), there are differences regarding 4 of the burials. Burials C°34-31, C°36-60 and C°40-76 are listed as female, while I classified them as male; the reverse is the case with C°36-6. Concerning the first three, it is interesting to note that cranial gracility is seemingly common among Hopewellian males, as compared to, say, Late Woodland males. Post-cranially, Hopewellian males possess what might be considered a normal degree of robusticity. This gracility might be attributable to the effects of deformation, but data is insufficient to support such a claim at this time; it can be noted, however, that these three males are cranially deformed, as are the males from the Norton Mounds which also demonstrate this lack of robusticity.

THE FREDERICK SITE

The Frederick site is located in Schuyler County, west central Illinois, and was excavated by Mr. Roderick Hiles from 1960 to 1962 (Young, 1960; Perkins, 1965). The skeletal material used in this study was excavated from mound 4, and is currently in the collections of the Indiana University Department of Anthropology. Sherds found in the mound fill were all Hopewellian, with neither Late Woodland nor Mississippian sherds being represented (Perkins, 1965:80).

The burial numbers associated with the six crania I measured at Indiana University have no apparent relationship to the burials listed by Perkins, so the identification of these burials as Hopewellian is an assumption. Five of the burials are males (11-SC-A, -1, -14, -20 and -21) and the sixth is a female (11-SC-48). In Perkins' report, burials 11-SC-A and 11-SC-48 are not mentioned, 11-SC-1 is reported to have been removed by vandals, 11-SC-20 was identified as a female, and 11-SC-21 was identified as a small child. No demographic data is available for the Frederick site. The metric data for the Frederick site burials is presented in Tables D1 and D3 of the Appendix.

THE SNYDERS MOUND GROUP

The Andrew Snyders Mound Group consists of 16 mounds running north and south along the edge of a bluff overlooking the Mississippi River in Calhoun County, Illinois, two miles north of Batchtown, Illinois. Several of the mounds were excavated by Walter Wadlo and Dr. P. F. Titterington in 1944 and 1945; Dr. Titterington's field notes, on file at the University of Michigan Museum of Anthropology, provide the extant information on this site. The remains of the skeletal material are in the United States National Museum, and include five males ($C^{o}104$-1, $C^{o}104$-4, $C^{o}111$-1, $C^{o}111$-2 and $C^{o}116$-1) and a female ($C^{o}104$-2) which were sufficiently complete to allow measurement; the collection also includes the fragmentary remains of 7 males and 4 females. The burials from $C^{o}104$ are from a subfloor pit, burials $C^{o}104$-1 and -2 being extended and $C^{o}104$-4 a bundle burial. The female, $C^{o}104$-2, had copper earspools, mica, beaver incisors and 152 shell beads in association. Additional indications of a Hopewellian affiliation for $C^{o}104$-2, and hence the other two burials from the same pit, consists of typical Hopewellian deformation and the removal of a large plaque of bone from the lambdoid region. Such plaque removal is common in the Norton Mounds Hopewellian skulls, and has also been reported from a burial in mound 5A, group B of the Utica Mounds in northern Illinois (Flanders, 1965:299).

No cultural information is available for C^{o}111-1 or C^{o}111-2, and C^{o}116-1 was found extended alongside a female, at original ground level, with, according to Titterington, "no associations to indicate cultural affiliations." Tables E1 and E3 of the Appendix contain the metric data from the Snyders site.

THE STEUBEN SITE

The Steuben Site, consisting of nine burial mounds and a village site, is located in Steuben Township, Marshall County, central Illinois (Morse, 1963). Mound 1, from which the extant skeletal material was recovered, has been dated at A.D. 390±250 (M-378) and A.D. 400±250 (M-380), and would thus represent a transitional time period between Middle and Late Woodland. On the basis of the artifacts, however, these dates are felt to be about 200 years too recent (Morse, 1963:114).

The sex and age distribution of the 58 individuals reported by Morse (1963:91) indicates that 15 of the 35 adults were males, 16 females and 4 were of indeterminate sex, the remaining 23 individuals being children under 14. Of the original 58 burials, 39 are currently in the collections of the University of Michigan Museum of Anthropology. Their state of preservation is extremely poor, as can be seen from the small amount of metric data in Tables F1, 2 and 3 of the Appendix. In an unpublished manuscript, Eyman (n.d.) indicated a close relationship between the pooled-sex Steuben series and those from the Turner site in southern Ohio (Hooton, 1922). The condition of the skeletal material prevents such a metric analysis of the sexes considered separately.

THE JUNTUNEN SITE

The Juntunen Site is located on Bois Blanc Island in the Straits of Mackinac, and was excavated by the University of Michigan Museum of Anthropology in the summers of 1960 and 1961 (McPherron, 1967). The site contains three Late Woodland cultural phases, with a time span of A.D. 800 to 1400, and a fourth component, known as feature 45 or the Arrowhead Drive site, is Middle Woodland, with human bone from the feature being dated at A.D. 60±120 (M-1392).

Of the 65 burials recovered, 57 are assignable to the latest Late Woodland phase, the Juntunen phase, while the remaining 8 burials are from the Middle Woodland feature 45 (McPherron, 1967:201). The Juntunen phase saw a shift in cultural orientation from Wisconsin in the preceding Bois Blanc phase, to the east and "incipient Iroquois-style pottery development (McPherron, 1967:297)."

The Juntunen skeletal material has been previously described (Eyman, 1964; Eyman and Bettarel, 1965), the results indicating that the feature 45 burials are very similar to those from the Norton Mounds, while the later burials are, not surprisingly, quite dissimilar to the Norton series. The Juntunen phase skeletal series has been associated with Ontario series, on the basis of the presence of ossuary interments.

The sex and age distribution for the burials from the Juntunen phase indicates the presence of 12 adult males, 5 adult females, 13 adults of indeterminate sex, 1 male, 1 female and an individual of unknown sex in the "transitional" age category, and 23 subadults.

An interesting feature noted in 10 of the adult and transitional-aged skulls is the removal of a large plaque of bone, located in the parietal area. Similar cranial alteration has been noted at the Younge site (Greenman, 1937) and the Riviere au Vase site (Fitting, 1965), both located in southeastern Michigan. Eyman and Bettarel point out that this post-mortem plaque removal is also common among the Norton burials, and associate it with the Huron head-piercer myth. Since the major cultural orientation of the Juntunen, Younge and Riviere au Vase sites is clearly to the east, an explanation of the plaque removal involving Huron or proto-Huron mythology is not unreasonable. Considering the Norton mounds cultural position, such an association is less clear. Also, the location of the plaque removal, as well as the techniques employed are very different, the similarity being restricted to the presence of a large opening in the skull.

The Late Woodland skeletal series from the Juntunen site is included here as a comparative series, to indicate the relationship, or lack thereof, between the earlier Norton series and later indigenous Michigan populations. The metric data for the Juntunen series is presented in Tables H1, 2 and 3 of the Appendix.

THE YOUNGE SITE

The Younge site is located in Goodland Township, Lapeer County, southeastern Michigan. The site is the subject of a monograph by Greenman, with a skeletal appendix by Byron O. Hughes (Greenman, 1937). The Younge site is representative of the Younge phase, the second of four phases in the Younge Tradition (Fitting, 1965:151). The Younge phase has a suggested time interval of A.D. 900 to 1100, the single radiocarbon date (M-1431) for this phase yielding a date of A.D. 1085±100 (Fitting, 1966). Like the Juntunen phase referred to above, the Younge site has definite cultural connections with Ontario, specifically with the Uren site in southwestern Ontario (Fitting, 1965:143).

A total of 88 burials were recovered from the site (Greenman, 1937:56-57), although the age distribution is based on a maximum of 74 individuals, including 39 males and 23 females (Greenman, 1937:127). Post-cranial measurements and observations were not taken in this study, because the post-cranial skeletons have become mixed in storage, and it is impossible to sort out individuals or sexes with any degree of certainty. The cranial measurements and male cranio-facial indices are presented in Tables I1 and I3 of the Appendix.

THE BACKLUND MOUND GROUP

The Backlund Mound Group consists of eight low mounds in Lake Township, Menominee County, in western Northern Michigan, (Fig. 1) three of which were excavated by the University of Michigan Museum of Anthropology in 1956 (Brose, 1968). All of the skeletal material was recovered from mound 5, the largest of the group. A total of 26 individuals was represented by the fragmentary skeletal material, including 12 males, 8 females, 5 children and a fetal ilium.

In terms of cultural connections,

> The Backlund Mound Group represents an archaeological complex previously unreported in Michigan. It is clearly understood only by reference to similar sites in northcentral and eastern Wisconsin. At Backlund we can see the contact of emergent Oneota with the northern Late Woodland Cultures which were spread from Lake Winnipeg to Mackinac across the Upper Great Lakes (Brose, 1968:49).

The Backlund skeletal material is included in this study primarily as a source of comparative data. In addition to the cultural differences between Backlund and the other sites utilized in this study, major morphological differences in the skeletal material are equally obvious. The Backlund series should therefore serve as a check on the efficacy of the statistical methods employed in this study to determine biological relationships. The morphological differences between the Backlund series and, for example, the Juntunen series, the latter being the most similar to Backlund in terms of culture, space and time,[1] are so obvious visually that it is to be expected that Backlund will be shown to be totally unrelated to any of the other series utilized in this study. The Backlund males are large and extremely robust, with broad, pentagonal skulls, unlike the more gracile, long-headed skulls characteristic of other Michigan Late Woodland populations. A comparison of Plates 1 and 2 shows the marked similarity between a typical Backlund male and an historic Chippewa skull from the United States National Museum collection. The cranial and post-cranial measurements, and the male cranio-facial indices taken on the Backlund skeletal material are listed in Tables J1, J2 and J3 in the Appendix.

THE BUSSINGER SITE

The Bussinger site is located in James Township, Saginaw County, east central Michigan. A University of Michigan Museum of Anthropology field crew worked at the site for several weeks in 1965, but the majority of the site was excavated by a number of amateur archaeologists, primarily Mr. Arthur Graves, of Saginaw, Michigan. Approximately 130 burials were excavated by Mr. Graves. The cultural remains indicate a long and continuous occupation at the site, from late Archaic to Late Woodland. The cultural material is presently being analyzed by John R. Halsey, of the University of North Carolina. The skeletal material utilized in the present study is all assignable to the Late Woodland component, which shares cultural similarities with both the Younge and Fort Wayne Mound sites (Halsey, 1968). The skeletal material should date around A.D. 1000 (J. R. Halsey, personal communication), which would be equivalent to the Younge phase date, but about 350 years later than the Fort Wayne Mound date of A.D. 750±120 (M-1843).

[1]A radiocarbon date was obtained from the femur of burial 7 from the Backlund site, the date being A.D. 1350±110 (M-1891).

The metric data from the Bussinger site burials is presented in Tables G1, G2 and G3 of the Appendix.

Several skeletal series taken from the literature are included for comparative purposes. These include the Middle Woodland Point Peninsula series from the Serpent Mound in Ontario (Anderson, 1968), the primary series from the Turner site in southern Ohio (Hooton, 1922), Neumann's Lenid and Ilinid series (Neumann, 1960; Robbins, 1968), the Fort Wayne Mound series from Wayne County, Michigan (Wilkinson, 1968) and Ohio Hopewell and Kentucky Adena series (Webb and Snow, 1945).

The Serpent Mounds site, located on Rice Lake, Peterborough County, Ontario, consists of nine mounds and a habitation component (Johnston, 1968:9). The burial goods and ceramics from the site indicate a close cultural relationship with Middle Woodland Point Peninsula sites from New York (Johnston, 1968:74). Two radiocarbon dates of A.D. 128±200 (M-850) and A.D. 302±150 (M-1105) confirm the Middle Woodland designation (Johnston, 1968:71).

The Lenid variety has been defined as the "distinctive physical type found in the Great Lakes Middle Archaic archaeological levels and persists in populations of the Early and Middle Hopewellian periods" (Robbins, 1968:22). The skeletal sample representing this variety consists of 45 adult male crania from Wisconsin Old Copper and Illinois Black Sand sites (ibid.). The Lenid variety is the same as that originally described by Neumann (1952*a*:16) as Otamid, although the Otamid were represented by 18 crania of the Karankawa on the Texas coast.

The Ilinid variety is "representative of Central Algonquian speakers such as the Miami and Menominee, and some Iroquoian speakers as the Seneca" (Robbins, 1968:32). Neumann originally referred to the Ilinids as Lenapids (Neumann, 1952*a*:23), and the description was based on 24 adult male skulls from the Maples Mills focus of southern Illinois. Robbins does not identify her Ilinid sample, other than noting it consists of 17 adult male skulls.

The skeletal material from the Fort Wayne Mound has been dated at A.D. 750±120 (M-1843) (Halsey, 1968:143), and is thus assignable to the early part of the Late Woodland period. Halsey (ibid.) notes that "ceramic relationships between the Fort Wayne Mound, Gibraltar, Bussinger and Riviere au Vase sites are very strong and other artifactual material . . . extended the relationships to the south and northeast," namely, Ohio and New York. The Gibraltar and Riviere au Vase sites are Late Woodland sites in southeastern Michigan.

The Ohio Hopewell skeletal material is from the Hopewell, Harness, Seip, Esch and Marietta sites (Webb and Snow, 1945: 288); the number of skulls from each site is not indicated. The Kentucky Adena skulls include all extant undeformed skulls (as of 1945) from Adena sites in Kentucky (Webb and Snow, 1945:247).

METHODOLOGY

SEX AND AGE DETERMINATION

The determination of sex was limited to adults. Individuals in their late teens represent the minimum sexing age, due to the lack of observable secondary sexual characteristics in younger individuals. The observations employed in determining sex are those of Hrdlicka (Stewart, 1952:127-34) for both the cranial and post-cranial skeleton. In the case of burials M1 and M6 from the Norton Mounds, both of which are indeterminate in terms of the standard cranial observations but definitely male post-cranially, a discriminant function formula (Giles and Elliot, 1963) was used on several measurements. The formula indicated that both skulls were male, and were in fact well above the 5 percent level established by Giles and Elliot.

Age estimates were based on a number of observations, including pubic symphyses (Stewart and McKern, 1957) dental development and eruption (Kronfeld, 1935; Meredith, 1946), epiphyseal union (Stevenson, 1924), endocranial suture closure (Todd and Lyon, 1924) and the degree of dental attrition. In most cases, all of these criteria could not be observed, and considering the amount of error inherent in some (Brooks, 1955; Stewart, 1962), rather inclusive age categories were employed. For the purposes of the biological distance statistics, it was necessary only to separate adults from subadults. While it is recognized that metric changes are involved in the aging process (see, for example, Allbrook, 1956; Baer, 1956; Goldstein, 1936; Garn, et al., 1967, 1968; Israel, 1967), the methods for determining the age of adults are generally too imprecise to adequately partition the adult skeletons into rigorous categories.

METRIC OBSERVATIONS

Unless otherwise noted, the measurements used in this study follow the procedures set forth by Hrdlicka (Stewart, 1952).

Abbreviations are those which will be used in the tables. A total of 26 measurements were taken on the cranio-facial skeleton and 18 on the post-cranial skeleton.

Cranio-facial measurements:

1. Maximum Length (L)
2. Maximum Breadth (B)
3. Minimum Frontal Breadth (MF)
4. Basion-Bregma Height (H)
5. Auricular Height (AH), the measurement was taken from bi-porion to bregma, using a head spanner
6. Endobasion-Nasion (BN)
7. Endobasion-Prosthion (BP)
8. Bizygomatic Breadth (BZ)
9. Nasion-Alveolar Point (NA)
10. Nasal Height (NH)
11. Nasal Width (NW)
12. Orbital Height (OH)
13. Orbital Width (OW), measured from maxillo-frontale to the lateral border of the orbit
14. Alveolar Length (AL)
15. Alveolar Width (AW), this measurement was taken externally, at the level of the second molar
16. Biporionic Width (BPW)
17. Biasterionic Width (BAW)
18. Minimum Length (ML), same as maximum length, but taken from nasion instead of glabella

19, 20. Left and Right Occipital Suture Length (LSL, RSL), these measurements taken from lambda to asterion, on both sides of the skull

21. Symphysis Height (SH)
22. Mandibular Body Length (BL), this measurement taken from the most anterior point of the mandible in the midline to gonion
23. Bigonial Breadth (BGB)
24. Bicondylar Breadth (BCB)
25. Ascending Ramus Height (RH)
26. Ascending Ramus Width (RW)

A series of 11 indices were calculated from several of these cranio-facial variables. The indices, with the abbreviations used in the tables of the Appendix, are as follows:

1. Cranial (L/B)
2. Height-Length (H/L)
3. Height-Breadth (H/B)
4. Fronto-Parietal (MF/B)
5. Cranio-Facial (BZ/B)
6. Cranial Module (L+B+H/3)
7. Orbital (OH/OW)
8. Nasal (NW/NH)
9. Upper Facial (NA/BZ)
10. Gnathic (BP/BN)
11. Zygo-Frontal (MF/BZ)

Post-cranial measurements:

1. Humerus: Maximum Length (HL)
2. Humerus: Maximum Head Diameter (HHD)
3. Humerus: Mid-shaft Anterior-Posterior Diameter (HA-P)
4. Humerus: Mid-shaft Medial-Lateral Diameter (HM-L)
5. Radius: Maximum Length (RL)
6. Ulna: Maximum Length (UL)
7. Clavicle: Maximum Length (CL)
8. Femur: Maximum Length (FL)
9. Femur: Bicondylar Length (FBL)
10. Femur: Maximum Head Diameter (FHD)
11. Femur: Sub-trochanteric Anterior-Posterior Diameter (FA'-P')

12. Femur: Sub-trochanteric Medial-Lateral Diameter (FM'-L')
13. Femur: Mid-shaft Anterior-Posterior Diameter (FA-P)
14. Femur: Mid-shaft Medial-Lateral Diameter (FM-L)
15. Tibia: Maximum Length (TL), this measurement taken from the tip of the medial malleolus to the proximal point of the intercondylar eminence
16. Tibia: Minimum Length (TL'), this measurement taken from the tip of the medial malleolus to the lateral condyle
17. Tibia: Nutrient Foramen Anterior-Posterior Diameter (TA-P)
18. Tibia: Nutrient Foramen Medial-Lateral Diameter (TM-L)

NON-METRIC OBSERVATIONS

The non-metric, or discontinuous, skeletal attributes listed below are included as another source of information which may clarify the biological relationships existing among the various groups included in this study. It is often felt that discontinuous traits are better predictors of genetic relationships than are continuous characteristics (Barry, 1968:128). The recording of discontinuous traits is accomplished either by using a presence-or-absence dichotomy, or the traits are categorized as slight, medium or marked. Yet not a few traits are characterized by being not simply absent or present, as they may be present in varying degrees of intensity, such traits having been termed "quasi-continuous" (Gruneberg, 1952). In some studies, only the present-absent categories are employed, when the traits are actually continuous when present (Laughlin and Jorgensen, 1956:7). Although the assumption that traits treated as discontinuous are more simply inherited than are continuous traits may be a logical one, the fact remains that we know no more about the inheritance of many discontinuous traits than we do about the inheritance of continuous traits.[2]

A concise statement of the nature of non-metric traits is offered by Barry (1968:108):

> . . . the underlying basis of the non-metrical variation is the resultant of a number of allelomorphs at different loci interacting to form (say) an organ rudiment which may be below the critical size for further development. If substitution at any one of these loci can affect the underlying rudiment so as to determine whether or not the threshold is overstepped, the trait in question will appear to be inherited in a simple ("Mendelian") fashion.

[2]There are, however, some exceptions (see Suzuki and Sakai, 1960; Johnson, Gorlin and Anderson, 1965; Selby, Garn and Kanareff, 1955).

The following traits were used in the non-metric analysis:

Pterion form
Epipteric bones
Mandibular tori
Auditory meatus exostoses
Palatine tori
Nasal profile
Nasal gutter
Wormian bones
Typanic dehiscences
Superior sagittal sinus direction
Parietal notch bone
Dental caries
Ante-mortem tooth loss

STATISTICAL PROCEDURES

Three statistical methods were employed in the analysis, in addition to the usual means, standard deviations and coefficients of variation. The first of these three, step-wise regression analysis, is described in the Discussion section of the present chapter. The other two procedures are those used to estimate the biological relationships, or distance, between the various populations.

The primary means utilized in the determination of biological distance is a step-wise discriminant analysis, BMDO7M (Dixon, 1968). This procedure has been used previously in a study of Indians of the southwest (Hanna, 1962) and of early populations from Japan (Howells, 1966). The computer program analyzes individuals in terms of their respective groups by computing the D^2 of Mahalanobis (Mahalanobis, 1936) of each individual from each group, and prints the posterior probability of each individual belonging to each group. As a means of graphically illustrating the relationships between groups, the computer program prints a two-dimensional graph of the first two canonical coefficients, or vectors. The canonical vectors reduce an N-dimensional space to two dimensions, where N is equal to the number of variables employed. These vectors account for 70 to 80 percent of the total variability encompassed in the N variables. The degree to which this percentage approaches 100 percent indicates the accuracy of the two coefficient. (See Rao, 1952:364-70 for the derivation of canonical vectors.)

The canonical coefficient graph is thus not totally accurate because of the differing amounts of variability left unaccounted for, and also because a multi-dimensional relationship is being treated as if it were two-dimensional. As a means of testing the significance of the various relationships illustrated by the canonical coefficients, between-group F-values are printed. Input for the program normally consisted of individual measurements, but in the case of populations taken from the literature where only means are available, a group can be treated as an individual for purposes of plotting. Such data are not used in the computation of discriminant functions or in tests of significant differences.

Since the input for the discriminant analysis program consists of individual measurements, the results will indicate primarily differences in size, rather than shape. The use of indices as estimators of shape distance is not warranted with this technique since the correlation and ratios between variables are considered by the computer program, and the variables themselves are not considered independently. It is also questionable whether indices are adequate representations of shape in the first place, since crania of markedly different shape could have identical indices.

As a means of considering differences and similarities due to shape, the metric data were analyzed with the use of profile patterns (Garn, Lewis and Walenga, 1968), using male cranial variables. The original variables are transformed into T-scores (McCall, 1939), having a mean of 50 and a standard deviation of 10. The degree of similarity of patterning of two populations was determined by calculating the correlation coefficient (r_T) between the variables of the two groups (Garn, Lewis and Walenga, 1968:1235).

The calculation of the T-scores is very simple, and can be easily accomplished on a desk calculator, using the formula

$$T = \frac{10(X_{i1} - \overline{X}_i)}{\overline{s}_i} + 50$$

where X_{i1} = the mean value of variable i in population 1,
$\overline{X}_i$ = the mean value of variable i in all populations,
and $\overline{s}_i$ = the mean standard deviation of variable i in all populations.

Although the profile pattern method is used here as a means of indicating relationships based on shape rather than size, it is clear that the T-scores themselves are not entirely independent of size. The more a single population deviates from the mean measurement, the higher or lower will be the T-score, relative to 50. The T-score then, reflects the extent of pattern similarity regardless of absolute size. The value r_T is based on the summation of relationships of the several measurements. The correlation coefficient may be considered an estimation of shape, instead of size, to the extent that it evaluates two populations on the basis of the direction of their deviancy from the mean, and not the magnitude of this deviancy. In this way a measurement for which two groups have means which are both greater or lower than the total mean will add a positive increment to the value of r_T. The formula for the product-moment correlation coefficient is as follows:

$$r_T = \frac{Sxy}{\sqrt{(Sx^2)(Sy^2)}}$$

where S = sum, and x and y are the deviations from the mean T-score in two populations, x and y.

DISCUSSION

It is often the case in studies of biological distance that little or no emphasis is given to the selection of variables to be used. Frequently, variables are selected because of the ease in taking the particular measurement, because the nature of the skeletal remains restrict the number and types of measurements, or because the measurements have been taken in previous studies. The results of this study indicate that quite different biological relationships emerge with the use of different sets of metric variables. The purpose, therefore, of this section is to discuss the different variables used, with emphasis on their heritability, variability and a method of increasing sample sizes.

THE HERITABILITY OF METRIC VARIABLES

The measurements taken in this study are more or less standard in osteometric studies. These, and others as well, are usually taken because of precedent, and not necessarily because they convey genetic information which is lacking in other measurements; the opposite may in fact be true. Factor analysis is one method which has been employed to serve as a rationale for choosing certain measurements as being those which most accurately describe a population (Howells, 1957; Landauer, 1962). Given these factors, there is still the question of what their basis might be (Driver, 1965; Vandenberg, 1962); that is, are the factors of the statistician equivalent to those of the geneticist?

Estimates of heritability have been made for certain anthropometric traits, with the results showing a considerable amount of variability, depending upon the method used to estimate heritability. One such method involves the study of twins. In general the intrapair differences between monozygous and dizygous twins are compared, and the assumption is made that differences between monozygous twins are the result of environmental effects, since the genetic content of each twin is identical. The heritability is often expressed as the F-ratio between dizygous and monozygous twin pairs, statistically significant F-values indicating significantly more variability within dizygous twin pairs than within identical pairs.

The results of these twin studies show a fairly high agreement (Vandenberg, 1962), in that certain traits such as stature, limb lengths, facial height and the cephalic index appear to be highly heritable, having little within-pair variability among dizygous twins (Clark, 1956; Osborne and DeGeorge, 1959; Ostertag, 1959; Hiernaux, 1963; Vandenberg and Strandskov, 1964). The low environmental influence on stature and the related limb lengths suggested in these studies is surprising considering the widespread trend of rapidly increasing stature in industrialized societies.

Some recent studies indicate that maximum stature has not, in fact, been increasing, but that there has been instead an increase in the growth rate (Boyne, 1960; Huber, 1968). This demonstration of the stability of maximum stature through time would supposedly indicate a low environmental component, thus offering confirmation of the results of the various twin studies mentioned above. Yet in the face of this type of evidence, there exists a considerably larger amount of evidence pointing to a high amount of environmental variance. Numerous studies on descendents of immigrants offer conclusive evidence that stature undergoes significant change concurrent with a change in environment (see, for example, Fishberg, 1905; Boas, 1911; Goldstein, 1943; Lasker, 1946; Kaplan, 1954). The very existence of these significant changes in stature among offspring of immigrants would seem to point to the fact that twin studies are not the best means of estimating heritability, especially concerning stature and limb lengths.

The assumption underlying the twin study method mentioned above also neglects the fact that twins share a very similar environment, so environmental variance will be low, and heritability mistakenly high (Falconer, 1964:183). A high heritability estimate in Osborne and DeGeorge's study might also be misleading because they used only twins over 18 years of age, which has the effect of ignoring differences which might exist in the rate of growth of each twin (Vandenberg, 1962:335). Such growth differences would have the result of decreasing the heritability estimate. Age-dependent growth differences must also be considered in comparing twins with their parents, as offspring-parent similarity shows a wide range of variability during the growth period of the children (Wolanski and Charzewska, 1967).

Despite the claim that certain twin studies show considerable agreement among themselves (Vandenberg, 1962:334), discrepancies do exist. Osborne and DeGeorge (1959) find the cephalic index to have the highest heritability among the variables tested, while the same trait is listed as "unstable," inferring a low heritability, in Ostertag's study (Ostertag, 1959). Falconer has estimated the heritability of stature, using the twin method, as 0.58 (Falconer, 1964:185), thereby falling within the range of heritabilities calculated by Pearson and Lee (1903:379), using offspring-parent regression. In a study mentioned above (Vandenberg and Strandskov, 1964), twins were compared in terms of 64 anthropometric traits, of which only 3 were *not* significant at or beyond the .05 level of probability. Of the remaining 61 variables all but 6 were significant (in terms of F-values) at or beyond the .01 level. This implies, of course, that nearly all anthropometric traits have very significant heritability factors, while being little influenced by environment. It is informative to note that the length of the left ear is significant at the .05 level (F=1.83), while the right ear shows a considerably more significant difference (P=.01) between mono- and dizygous twins (F= 11.45).

Given such difficulties and inexplicable results, it would seem that the regression of the offspring on the parents, or on one of the parents, should yield more reliable estimates of heritability (Falconer, 1964:169). An early study using the offspring-parent regression method found three anthropometric traits—stature, arm span and forearm length—to have an estimated heritability of about .5 (Pearson and Lee, 1903:378). These traits are precisely those which the various twin studies mentioned above indicated have very low environmental variance. The heritability studies thus point to three very different conclusions: First, that anthropometric characters have varying heritabilities; second, that most characters have a high amount of heritability; and, finally, that several characters that have been tested have similar, but lower, heritability estimates.

VARIABILITY OF METRIC CHARACTERS

It was originally felt that mandibular measurements could be excluded from the determination of biological distance because of the action of muscles of mastication on the mandible (Washburn,

1947; Scott, 1957). If behavior does play an important part in the morphology of the mandible, then the mandibular measurements which are related to the affected areas of the mandible should show greater variation than, say, measurements of the cranial vault. To examine this situation, coefficients of variation were calculated for cranial, facial and mandibular measurements derived from the series used in this study, Indians from the Southwest (Hooton, 1930), Alaskan Eskimos (Wolpoff, 1968), California Indians (Hrdlicka, 1906), the Indian Knoll population (Snow, 1948) and Neumann's Dakotid and Lenid series (Neumann, 1952*b*).

A graphic representation of the coefficients of variation is presented in Figure 2. What emerges from this comparison is that there is a clear progression of increasing variability as one moves from the vault to the face and finally to the mandible. Of the six mandibular variables, the height of the symphysis, ascending ramus height and ascending ramus width show clear peaks of high variability. In a more extensive study, de Villiers found 10 of 13 mandibular variables to have coefficients of variation in the "high" range, or above 6.0 (de Villiers, 1968:79).

It is also interesting to note the high coefficient of variation of nasal width. In all of the series utilized in this comparison, from Eskimos to Indians of the southwest, this elevation of the nasal width variability was observed. That this is not an isolated phenomenon is further indicated by the fact that similarly high variability of nasal width has been recorded in several Sub-saharan African populations (Hiernaux, 1968; de Villiers, 1968).

The high variability of nasal width and of some of the mandibular variables has been explained as due to the nature of the coefficient of variation, in that a small measurement will result in a large coefficient, since the measurement forms the divisor of the equation, $C.V. = 100s/\bar{X}$, where *s* is the standard deviation (de Villiers, 1968:75). Yet there are some exceptions, such as the orbital and palatal measurements, for which the coefficients of variation are not particularly large despite the small means involved. Also, since the coefficient of variation is a relative expression, a large value does indicate a relatively large standard deviation, and hence variability.

A second explanation is that offered by Pearson and Davin (1924:346), who point out that a coefficient of variation will be lower among variables which encompass more than one anatomical unit—such as cranial length—than among single unit variables. Finally, it has been suggested that those variables with the

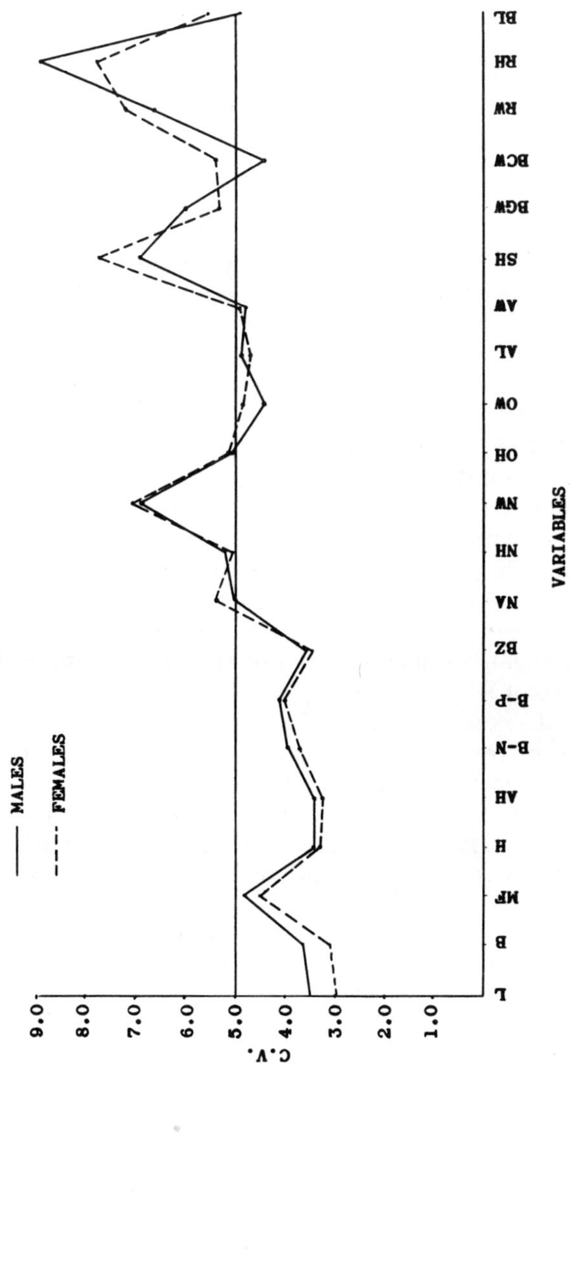

FIG. 2. Coefficients of variation.

higher variability are those which are more subject to environmental adaptation (Hiernaux, 1968:24). Considering the high coefficients of variation of the face as compared to the vault, it is interesting to note that the major changes in hominid cranial morphology during the past 200,000 years have occurred in the facial region, presumably in response to selection (Brace, 1962: 349; Brace and Montagu, 1965:264). Coefficients of variation thus might provide us with additional information concerning the problems of heritability referred to in the previous section.

As the variability of certain measurements increases within groups, it becomes impossible to differentiate two groups, provided the means of the variables are not radically different. If such is the case, then we may have evidence of similar adaptive responses occurring within different, and possibly unrelated, groups. It is also evident that groups will be more readily differentiated statistically when less variable measurements are used, as will be shown in Chapter II.

No significant differences in coefficients of variation between males and females could be detected, although Figure 2 indicates that females are slightly less variable than males in the major vault and cranial base measurements. The mean coefficient of variation, for 21 variables, was 4.97 in males and 4.96 in females. A somewhat more pronounced trend in this direction is detectable among certain groups from South Africa (de Villiers, 1968:236-45). The cause of this slight difference is unclear, but a relationship to sex-linkage is a possibility (Garn, Rohmann and Hertzog, 1969).

The sex differences observable in de Villiers' study, and in fact the major differences in variability in general, would seem to be related also to the sequential growth in the areas concerned. The increasing coefficients of variability noted as one moves from the vault to the face and finally the mandible parallel the intensity of the adolescent growth spurt in these same regions:

> Whether (the brain) has any adolescent spurt is doubtful, although the issue cannot be decided on present data. . . . The face follows a curve midway between that of the top portion of the skull and the remainder of the skeleton. It is nearer its mature dimensions at birth and later than is body length, but still has a considerable adolescent spurt, which is greatest in the mandible (Tanner, 1964:310).

Similar relationships between the three regions were noted by Goldstein (1936:59) and in an earlier study by Tanner (1962:14-16).

The marked peak of variability in ramus height indicated in Figure 2 is predictable from the amount of adolescent growth spurt occurring in the ramus; by 12 years of age in males, 93 to 94 percent of the total growth is completed in the cranial base, as opposed to only 75 percent in ramus height (Tanner, 1964:16). The high variability in nasal width is puzzling, since the nasal width has a very slight growth spurt as compared to facial lengths (Goldstein, 1936:52). Yet despite the lack of a marked spurt, the coefficient of variation for nasal width does continue to increase from ages 3 to 21 (Goldstein, 1936:64), and while head form, as measured by the cephalic index, decreases in variability during this time period, nasal form shows an increasing variability (Goldstein, 1936:72).

The slightly lower variability in females as compared to males might be due to the observed differences in the time and intensity of the adolescent growth spurt. Females begin their adolescent spurt earlier than in males, and it is less intense (Tanner, 1964:322). If we can equate higher variability with a more intense growth spurt, as seems to be the case with most of the variables in Figure 2, then the male-female differences in this growth spurt might account for the differences in variability.

THE USE OF REGRESSION ANALYSIS IN DATA PREDICTION

An obvious problem in assessing biological relationships between populations utilizing metric data arises from the inability to make all observations on all individuals. Absence of or damage to certain skeletal landmarks is the major cause of missing data, but natural and artificial deformation also effectively eliminate certain measurements, depending on the location and severity of the deformation.

The degree to which certain measurements cannot be taken varies from population to population, the Illinois material (Knight, Snyders, Frederick and Klunk sites) being considerably more complete than the other samples. The Knight, Snyders and Frederick skeletal series were apparently selected on the basis of their preservation, as the available skeletal material represents only a fraction of the total number of burials at these sites. The Klunk material is similarly incomplete, as I selected the material on this basis as well. Time, and a prior commitment of the material to Hunter, did not allow an examination of the more than 300 individuals from the Klunk Mounds, thus observations were made on only the most complete adults. The skeletal series from Michigan are complete in terms of numbers of individuals recovered, but incomplete in terms of skeletal parts available for observation.

Faced with the problem of incomplete data in skeletal series which are small to begin with, it was necessary to include as many individuals in the analysis as possible. To make use of those skeletons which are incomplete one must either use only those variables which afford the maximum number of observations in all skeletal series, substitute group means for the missing data, or attempt to predict the missing variables from those that are present.

The first alternative, omitting those variables which are most often missing, results in a loss of information from certain areas, notably the facial skeleton, to a greater degree than from others. This procedure leads to a reduction in sample size, which can hardly be afforded given the small sample sizes available. Finally, the selection of variables on the basis of their frequencies partially precludes their selection on any other basis. While we know little or nothing of the genetic basis underlying most anthropometric variables, omitting the least frequently measureable variables in favor of those more readily obtainable can only further prevent an understanding of this genetic basis.

The substitution of group means for missing variables would naturally tend to produce an artificial homogeneity within a sample, and thereby magnify any real differences that might exist between two populations. Despite this major shortcoming, this method is often used as a means of increasing sample sizes.

A third alternative in dealing with missing data is that of predicting the missing values by regression analysis, and this is the procedure utilized in this study. The prediction was accomplished by using a step-wise multiple regression analysis program, BMDO2R (Dixon, 1968). The samples used in this program were based on sex, age (adult) and site, with 22 craniofacial and 18 post-cranial variables being utilized (cranio-facial and post-cranial variables were run separately). The program adds one variable to the regression equation at each step, the variable added being the one which has the highest partial correlation with the dependent variable and similarly the highest F-value. An original run was made in which all variables were forced; in terms of cranial variables, 20 steps were specified in order to determine the maximum number of significantly correlated variables for each of the 20 original variables. The maximum number of significantly correlated variables varies with the number of individuals available, the maximum being 5 predicting variables with the largest complete series, 15 males from the Knight Mounds. Originally, a correlation program for samples with missing data was run which allowed the use of 24 Knight male crania; here six was the maximum number of significantly correlated independent variables for any one dependent variable. The correlation coefficients of the 20 cranial and 6 mandibular variables, derived from all males from all sites, are presented in Table 4.

As the sample size decreases, the predicting ability, in terms of the number of predicting variables, decreases as well. These remaining variables retain their statistical significance, however, as noted by their F-values. A serious limitation of the program is that all input data must be complete, thus only those skulls from which all measurements could be taken could be used to determine the regressions. This imposed a rather drastic selection on many of the samples, as at least five complete individuals are necessary to produce a sufficient number of predicting variables. In order to predict missing variables in those individuals from the smaller series it was necessary to pool all adults from all sites, keeping the sexes separate. This procedure has the effect of minimizing the differences between groups in the discriminant analysis, and should make most groups relatively more similar to the Knight and Klunk series, since these latter groups contain more complete data, and thus play a large part in the model from which the regression is drawn.

An examination of the residuals—the differences between the observed and predicted values—indicates the accuracy of the regression method as a solution to missing data problems. Table 5 lists the means, standard deviations and mean residuals for 17 cranio-facial variables taken on 41 males and 15 females. Both samples were pooled, with individuals from several sites included, although the male sample is more heterogeneous than the female, due to differences in the availability of complete crania. This difference in homogeneity is reflected in the marked differences between male and female residuals. That the females are considerably more predictable than the males is due primarily to the greater homogeneity of the female sample;[3] an inspection of the standard deviations affirms this similarity.

[3]This homogeneity is assumed, in that the female sample represents fewer cultural components than the male sample.

TABLE 4

CORRELATION COEFFICIENTS OF 26 CRANIAL VARIABLES

	L	B	MF	H	AH	B-N	B-P	BZ	NA	NH	NW	OH	OW
L	-	.150	.330*	.224	.159	.419*	.598†	.307*	.302†	.103	.022	.022	.267*
B		-	.460†	.300*	.320†	.205	-.053	.679†	.132	.091	.102	.095	-.015
MF			-	-.059	.021	.249*	.114	.546†	.185	.103	.166	.273*	.335†
H				-	.762†	.203	.083	.067	.356†	.419†	-.044	.170	.073
AH					-	.103	.157	.111	.312†	.245	-.128	.228	-.029
B-N						-	.419†	.411†	.253*	.247*	.156	.112	.313†
B-P							-	.088	.150	-.011	.085	-.142	.134
BZ								-	.243*	.217	.309†	.176	.359†
NA									-	.518†	-.182	.225	.299†
NH										-	.038	.526†	.396†
NW											-	-.020	.183
OH												-	.202
OW													-

	AL	AW	BPW	BAW	ML	LSL	RSL	SH	BL	BGW	BCW	RH	RW
L	.236*	.168	.184	.293*	.969†	.461†	.374†	.039	.318†	.253*	.374†	.090	.374†
B	-.061	.155	.848†	.634†	.100	.262*	.246*	-.075	.134	.258*	.507†	.227	.249*
MF	-.031	.058	.439†	.380†	.298*	.258*	.262*	-.101	.211	.325†	.383†	.042	.129
H	.006	.394†	.363†	.253*	.181	.268*	.193	.178	.236*	.035	.193	.197	.022
AH	-.040	.311†	.387†	.336†	.120	.341†	.274	.293*	.168	-.062	.196	.237	-.029
B-N	.086	.094	.233*	.087	.395†	.062	.005	.147	.358†	.279*	.278*	.312†	.335†

TABLE 4 (Continued)

	AL	AW	BPW	BAW	ML	LSL	RSL	SH	BL	BGW	BCW	RH	RW
B-P	.680†	.288*	.012	.180	.554†	.210	.145	.220	.184	.023	.166	.172	.320†
BZ	.074	-.198	.747†	.367†	.273*	.123	.029	.131	.519†	.455†	.702†	.416†	.385†
NA	.200	.432†	.123	.114	.264*	.211	.138	.484†	.293†	.031	.144	.303*	.046
NH	-.005	.229	.105	-.014	.109	.056	.039	.239*	.143	.083	.078	.256*	.000
NW	.084	.038	.125	-.008	-.009	-.180	-.237*	-.116	.243*	.116	.320†	-.041	.065
OH	-.126	.095	.158	-.002	.062	.069	.047	-.031	.136	.103	.140	.086	-.011
OW	.147	.098	.002	.042	.245	-.035	-.050	.240*	.177	.196	.193	.240*	.034
AL	-	.233*	.017	.136	.200	-.051	-.090	.304†	.065	.024	.130	.142	.177
AW		-	.247*	.164	.126	.110	.134	.265*	.271*	-.042	.164	.169	-.003
BPW			-	.637†	.133	.228	.215	-.039	.207	.376†	.613†	.256*	.259*

	BAW	ML	LSL	RSL	SH	BL	BGW	BCW	RH	RW
BAW	-	.270*	.470†	.562†	-.119	.003	.209	.258*	.112	.129
ML		-	.491†	.408†	.065	.624†	.228	.346†	.091	.388*
LSL			-	.833†	-.031	.182	-.012	.066	.218	.223
RSL				-	-.103	.104	-.014	.041	.163	.135
SH					-	.119	-.069	.104	.375†	.056
BL						-	.203	.353†	.260*	.328*
BGW							-	.522†	.027	.132
BCW								-	.175	.244*
RH									-	.277*
RW										-

*p = .05; † = .01.

TABLE 5

MEAN RESIDUALS FOR 17 CRANIO-FACIAL VARIABLES

	Males (N=41)			Females (N=15)		
Var.	Mean	S.D.	Residual	Mean	S.D.	Residual
L	181.0	6.70	1.83	174.3	4.59	0.27*
B	141.2	6.85	2.48	135.1	3.96	0.87
MF	94.1	4.43	1.80	91.2	3.61	1.06
H	142.5	6.43	2.59	137.0	5.42	0.18
AH	123.6	5.06	2.16	119.5	5.71	0.19
B-N	105.9	4.76	2.41	100.5	2.75	0.37
B-P	101.2	4.49	1.48	97.5	3.60	0.42
BZ	143.5	5.56	1.65	130.9	4.96	0.34
NA	73.4	3.66	1.78	69.9	4.63	0.34
NH	53.3	2.46	1.36	50.9	2.33	0.32
NW	26.6	2.16	1.27	25.6	1.76	0.40
OH	35.6	2.02	1.11	35.3	1.71	0.28
OW	43.6	1.97	0.84	42.3	1.29	0.34
AL	53.6	2.97	1.48	51.9	2.56	0.39
AW	66.0	2.91	1.72	63.8	2.70	0.71
BPW	125.8	5.77	1.58	117.9	5.15	0.72
BAW	111.9	4.83	1.63	107.1	3.27	0.63

*This residual is unrealistically small, and is due to the fact that maximum length here is being predicted by minimum length (measured from nasion). Minimum length was removed from the calculation of male residuals, and the female maximum length residual should be more in the range of that of the males.

One assumption necessary for the use of this method of data prediction is that the regressions of the several variables are linear. This linearity, or approximate linearity, has been demonstrated for some anthropometric traits (Mahalanobis, Majumdar and Rao, 1949, cited by Hanna, 1962:502). Despite this unproven assumption of regression linearity, and the heterogeneity of the male sample, the fact that the residuals are only a fraction of the standard deviations further affirms the accuracy of the predictions. Given a population from a single site and time period, thereby reducing the variability of the measurements, the prediction of missing data would be expected to be better than in the present study.

As a further demonstration of the accuracy of the regression analysis, the residuals for the pooled male series in Table 5 were compared with the differences between values obtained by two observers measuring the same skeletal series. In the first case, the series measured consisted of 12 adult males from a single site; methods of measurement were supposedly identical,[4] as were the calipers used by both observers. As can be seen in Table 6, the regression-produced residuals are smaller than the observed differences in the case of six variables, larger in seven and equal in the remaining variable.

TABLE 6

COMPARISON OF RESIDUALS AND OBSERVED DIFFERENCES

	Observer I	Observer II		
Var.	Mean	Mean	Difference	Residual*
L	182.0	183.0	1.00	1.83
B	139.1	138.7	0.40	2.48
MF	97.5	95.6	1.90	1.80
H	135.15	132.9	2.25	2.59
B-N	100.4	102.8	2.40	2.41
B-P	97.1	100.3	3.20	1.48
BZ	139.3	137.1	2.20	1.65
NA	72.0	71.5	0.50	1.78
NH	52.5	52.4	0.10	1.36
NW	25.5	25.8	0.30	1.27
OH	34.5	35.3	0.80	1.11
OW	40.1	43.0	2.90	0.84
AL	54.8	53.25	1.55	1.48
AW	64.6	64.7	0.10	1.72

*From males, Table 5.

The second comparison is based on the differences observed in the results of measurements taken by Hughes (Greenman, 1937) and me on the Younge site skeletal material. The method of comparison is somewhat different than in the previous comparison, which might account for the differences in the results (see Table 7). In the Younge series the measurements were compared by individual instead of comparing the means for each measurement as in the first case. Concerning the males, Table 7 shows that the predicted measurements, as indicated by the mean residuals, are in general slightly larger than the mean differences, but considerably smaller than some of the individual differences, as indicated by the range of differences.

[4]Both observers reportedly used Hrdlicka's methods of measurement (Stewart, 1952), but the differences in the values obtained must be due to individual variations from these methods.

TABLE 7

COMPARISONS OF MEASUREMENTS ON CRANIA FROM THE YOUNGE SITE
(In Millimeters)

Variable	Males				Females			
	Number of Comparisons	Range of Differences	Mean Difference	Mean Residual	Number of Comparisons	Range of Differences	Mean Difference	Mean Residual
L	10	-1 to +4	1.20	1.83	7	-3 to +1	1.43	0.27
B	12	-4 to +2	1.17	2.48	6	-1 to +2	1.00	0.87
MF	11	-3 to 0	0.91	1.80	5	0 to +2	0.80	1.06
H	12	-2 to +1	0.83	2.59	8	-6 to +1	2.00	0.18
B-N	11	-6 to +4	1.64	2.41	6	-3 to +2	1.33	0.37
B-P	6	-1 to +3	1.33	1.48	5	-2 to +8	2.60	0.42
BZ	5	-2 to +1	1.40	1.65	3	-1 to 0	0.33	0.34
NA	5	-1 to +1	0.60	1.78	5	0 to +5	2.20	0.34
NH	5	0 to +2	1.20	1.36	5	-6 to +1	1.80	0.32
NW	6	-1 to +1	0.67	1.27	4	0 to +2	1.00	0.40
OH	6	-1 to +4	1.00	1.11	5	-1 to +1	0.60	0.28
AL	4	-7 to +5	5.00	1.48	3	+1 to +5	3.89	0.39
AW	5	-1 to +4	2.20	1.72	1	0	0.00	0.71

Although this method should be expanded to encompass larger samples, the indication is that the regression analysis procedure is at least as reliable as the use of published material. It is informative to note that I classified as female 5 of the Younge burials which are considered male by Hughes, while the reverse is true in the case of two which I consider to be male. In addition, several of the burials in Hughes' tables apparently no longer exist, while I list some which are missing in Hughes' report. This information is presented not as a condemnation, but instead to indicate the care which must be taken when using published material in skeletal analyses, and in fact raises some questions as to the validity of using previously published material at all.

II

RESULTS

THIS section of the study contains the results of the statistical procedures utilized in the comparison of the several skeletal series. First the results of the discriminant analyses will be presented, followed by the T-score analyses and correlation coefficients, and finally the comparison of the non-metric attributes by means of the Chi-square test.

DISCRIMINANT FUNCTION ANALYSIS

The results of the discriminant analyses are illustrated in Figures 3 through 11, each of which will be described in detail below. These illustrations involve the two-dimensional plotting of the mean canonical coefficients for the particular groups involved in each analysis. The spatial relationships between the various group means are an indication of the biological distances between the various groups. The presence of a dashed line between any two group means indicates a statistically significant difference at or beyond the .01 probability level, as determined by an F-test. While the absence of a dashed line does not imply a statistically significant similarity, the relative proximity of two groups is an adequate indication of a similarity in their respective measurements. The relative similarity or lack thereof between the various groups in the discriminant analyses is primarily an expression of size relationships, as opposed to those based on shape.

It is the usual practice in studies of biological distance to base the conclusions on a single analysis using various combinations of cranial, facial, mandibular and, occasionally, post-cranial variables. This study will depart from this technique, and will consider the various skeletal regions separately, as well as in combination. By treating the analysis in this fashion, it is hoped that a more meaningful statement of the observed similarities and dissimilarities can be made, in terms of locating the areas of these similarities and differences.

EIGHTEEN CRANIO-FACIAL VARIABLES (FIG. 3)

The first discriminant analysis is based on 18 cranio-facial variables and 6 skeletal series. This analysis resulted in a wide spread in terms of distances, and in a relatively large number of significant differences. As can be seen in Figure 3, the Norton series is significantly different from all of the other five groups, Klunk from all but Knight, and Juntunen from all but Younge. While it is evident that the Norton series is closer to the two Illinois series than it is to the Late Woodland groups from Michigan, it should be emphasized that Norton is significantly different from these Illinois groups.

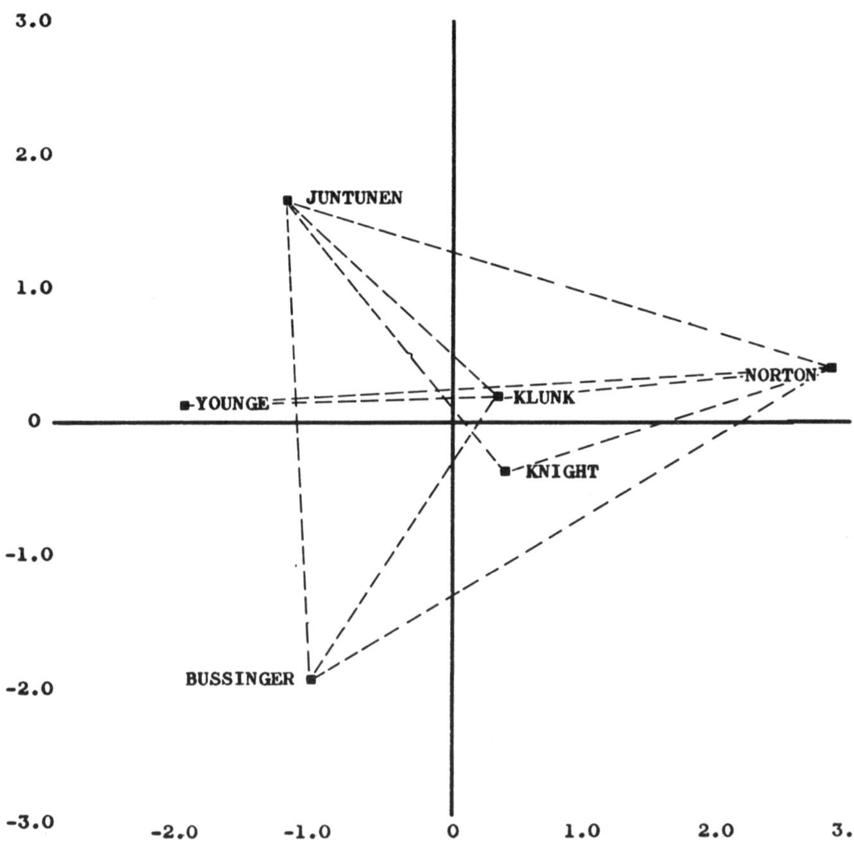

FIG. 3. Canonical Coefficients of 18 Cranio-Facial Variables.

The distances suggested in Figure 3 are not too meaningful however, because of the large number of variables relative to the total sample size of 70 male crania. Of the 18 variables used in this analysis, the discrimination is based primarily on 6 variables. These variables, in order of decreasing discriminatory value, are OH, AH, B, H, ML and MF.

Table 8 indicates the accuracy of the classification of individuals into their respective archaeological groups. The table indicates a fairly high degree of accuracy, as most individuals

TABLE 8

CLASSIFICATION MATRIX: 18 CRAINIO-FACIAL VARIABLES

	Norton	Knight	Klunk	Bussinger	Juntunen	Younge	Ratio
Norton	6	1	0	0	0	0	6/7
Knight	0	15	2	2	1	2	15/22
Klunk	0	1	14	1	0	0	14/16
Bussinger	0	0	1	7	0	0	7/8
Juntunen	0	1	1	0	8	0	8/10
Younge	0	0	0	0	0	7	7/7

were classified correctly. For example, all crania which I designated as Younge crania were classified as such by the program. The Knight series was the least accurately classified, as 7 of the 22 Knight crania were placed in other series. The accuracy of the classification also gives an indication of the variability within each series, as series with low variability would tend to be correctly classified to a greater degree than highly variable series, provided, of course, that the means are reasonably similar.

SEVEN VAULT VARIABLES (FIG. 4)

The second run of the discriminant analysis program was made using 7 vault variables (H, B, L, B-P, B-N, BZ and MF) and the same 6 skeletal series as in the first analysis. As compared to Figure 3, the distances between groups in Figure 4 have diminished somewhat, as has the number of significant differences. The Norton series is still distinct, but is no longer significantly different from the Knight series. The Knight and

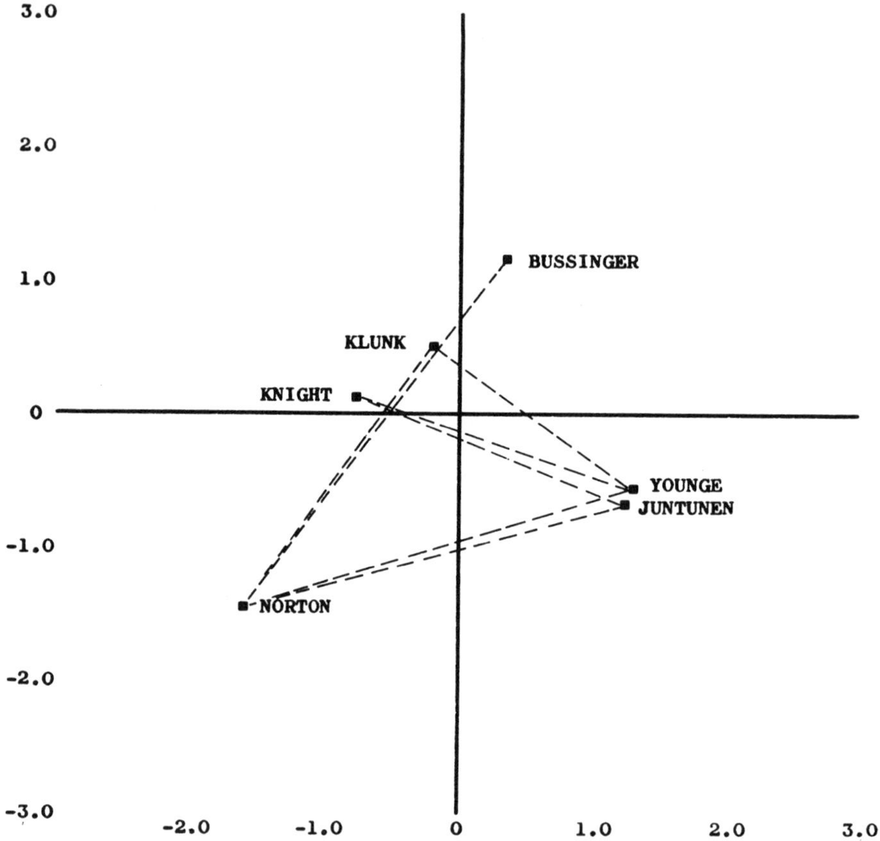

FIG. 4. Canonical Coefficients of 7 Vault Variables.

Klunk series remain close, as they were in Figure 3. The intermediate position of the Younge series, falling as it does between Juntunen and Bussinger in Figure 3 has changed, as the Juntunen and Younge series are very close in Figure 4. The Bussinger group, while still somewhat isolated, retains its lack of difference with Knight, and is also no longer significantly different from 4 of the 5 other series as well. Although the Bussinger series is spatially closer to the Knight and Klunk groups in Figure 4 than to Juntunen and Younge, it should be pointed out that it is not significantly different from these latter two series. Figure 4 thus indicates three rather distinct groupings, with Knight, Klunk and Bussinger in one, Juntunen and Younge in another, and Norton remaining isolated as the third.

TABLE 9

CLASSIFICATION MATRIX: 7 VAULT VARIABLES

	Norton	Knight	Klunk	Bussinger	Juntunen	Younge	Ratio
Norton	5	1	0	0	0	1	5/7
Knight	2	14	1	2	3	0	14/22
Klunk	0	4	9	3	0	0	9/16
Bussinger	0	1	2	6	0	1	6/10
Juntunen	0	0	0	1	6	3	6/10
Younge	0	0	2	1	3	6	6/11

The classification matrix presented in Table 9 verifies the decreasing differences between the various groups, as the accuracy of classification is less than that noted in Table 8.

SEVEN FACIAL VARIABLES (FIG. 5)

The third run is based on 7 facial variables (OW, AW, OH, AL, NW, NA and NH), with the same six skeletal series as in the first two runs. The biological distances, in terms of canonical coefficients, are represented in Figure 5. This illustration shows quite clearly the continuation of diminishing distances and loss of significant differences which was observed in Figure 4, as compared to Figure 3. Norton remains somewhat isolated, but its similarity (or lack of dissimilarity) is now with two of the Late Woodland groups from Michigan, Juntunen and Bussinger. Norton is significantly different from both of the Illinois series (Knight and Klunk) as well as the Younge series.

The Bussinger group remains somewhat problematical, as it is not significantly different from any of the other series, yet it is spatially removed from all of them in Figure 5. While Klunk and Knight retain their similarity, Juntunen and Younge are now significantly different. The proximity of the Juntunen series to the two Illinois groups is very surprising, considering the fact that these groups are the most geographically separate.

The classification matrix (Table 10) indicates the overall similarity between the various groups. Younge and Norton remain quite distinct, as 5 of 7 and 5 of 8 crania were classified correctly from these sites, respectively. Knight and Klunk show very little classification accuracy, as only 10 of 23 Knight crania

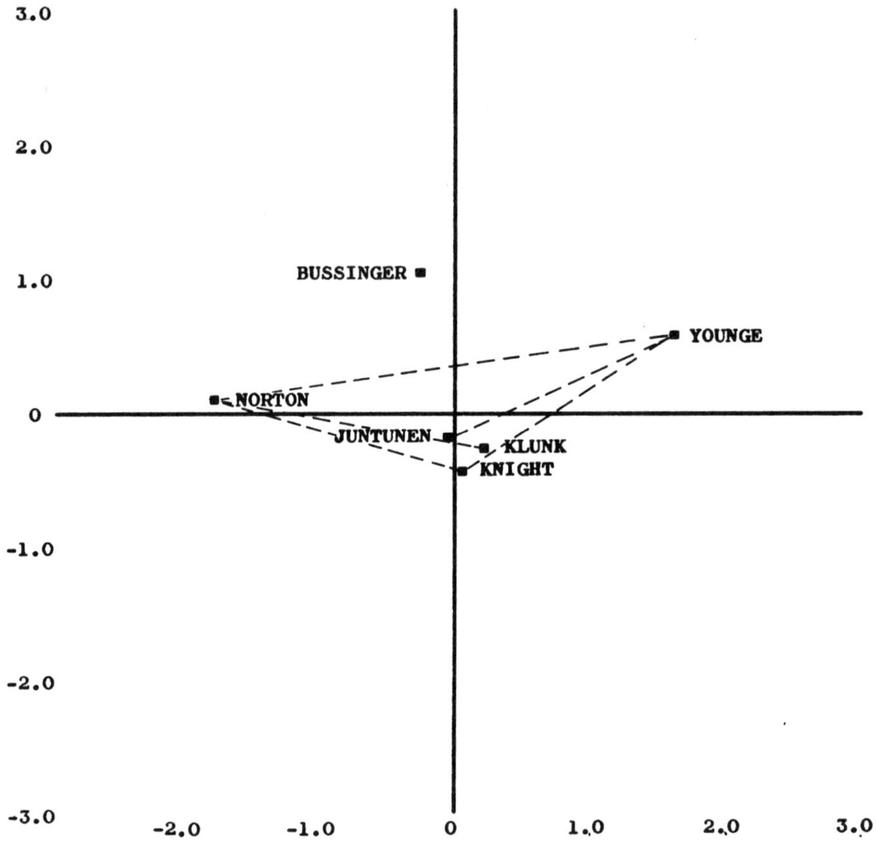

FIG. 5. Canonical Coefficients of 7 Facial Variables.

TABLE 10

CLASSIFICATION MATRIX: 7 FACIAL VARIABLES

	Norton	Knight	Klunk	Bussinger	Juntunen	Younge	Ratio
Norton	5	1	0	2	0	0	5/8
Knight	2	10	4	2	4	1	10/23
Klunk	1	4	5	4	3	2	5/19
Bussinger	1	0	1	6	1	0	6/9
Juntunen	0	2	2	3	4	0	4/11
Younge	0	0	1	1	0	5	5/7

were classified as such, and only 5 of 19 from the Klunk group were classified correctly. Although Norton was similar to Bussinger and Juntunen in Figure 5, Table 10 indicates that the Norton-Bussinger relationship is closer than the Norton-Juntunen relationship. This Norton-Bussinger relationship is much more in accord with archaeological data than that between Norton and Juntunen.

SIX MANDIBULAR VARIABLES (FIG. 6)

Six mandibular variables, SH, BL, BGW, BCW, RH and RW were used in the fourth discriminant analysis, and again the original six series were used. Figure 6 indicates the biological distances. As compared to the previous analyses, the number of significant differences has been reduced to only one, that between the Knight and Bussinger series. In addition, the spatial relationships have also diminished. It would appear from the results of this analysis that mandibular variables, or at least those used here, are not useful by themselves as population discriminators.

Disregarding the lack of significance for the moment, it is interesting to note that the relationships agree quite well with the temporal and spatial relationships of the various sites. Thus the three Late Woodland sites, Juntunen, Bussinger and Younge, are quite close to each other, as are the two Hopewellian series, Norton and Klunk. The single Illinois Late Woodland site, Knight, is the most isolated. Whether this particular arrangement in Figure 6 is simply fortuitous or perhaps meaningful is impossible to determine. All that can be said is that only Knight and Bussinger are significantly different, and that no other analysis based on other variables yields a comparable arrangement. Also, the associations suggested in Figure 6 could be due to factors other than biological (genetic) relatedness. The high variability of some of the mandibular variables has been alluded to previously, and this variability, whatever its causes, would reduce the chances of yielding significant differences and tend to make the groups appear similar.

ELEVEN CRANIAL INDICES (FIG. 7)

As mentioned previously, the use of cranial indices in conjunction with cranial measurements is not warranted in an analysis such as this, primarily because of the redundancy involved

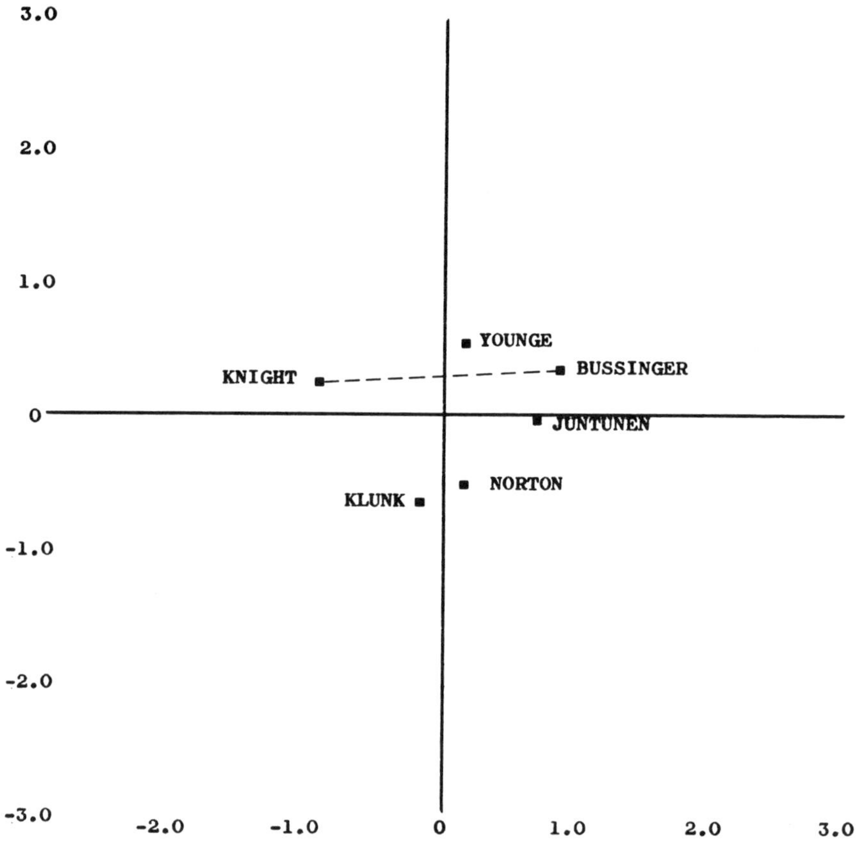

FIG. 6. Canonical Coefficients of 6 Mandibular Variables.

in the combined use of measurements and indices. To the extent that the use of indices alone as input data is permissible, it was felt that such an approach might suggest different relationships. Figure 7 illustrates these relationships among the same six skeletal series used in the previous analyses.

The extent to which the indices repeat the information contained in the metric variables is readily apparent in Figure 7. Thus in terms of distances, the Norton series is once again isolated from the others, in this case being significantly different from all but the Knight series. The Juntunen-Younge grouping is again obvious, and the Knight-Klunk-Bussinger relationship is very similar to that observed in Figure 4. The overall resemblance between Figures 7 and 4, the latter being based on 7

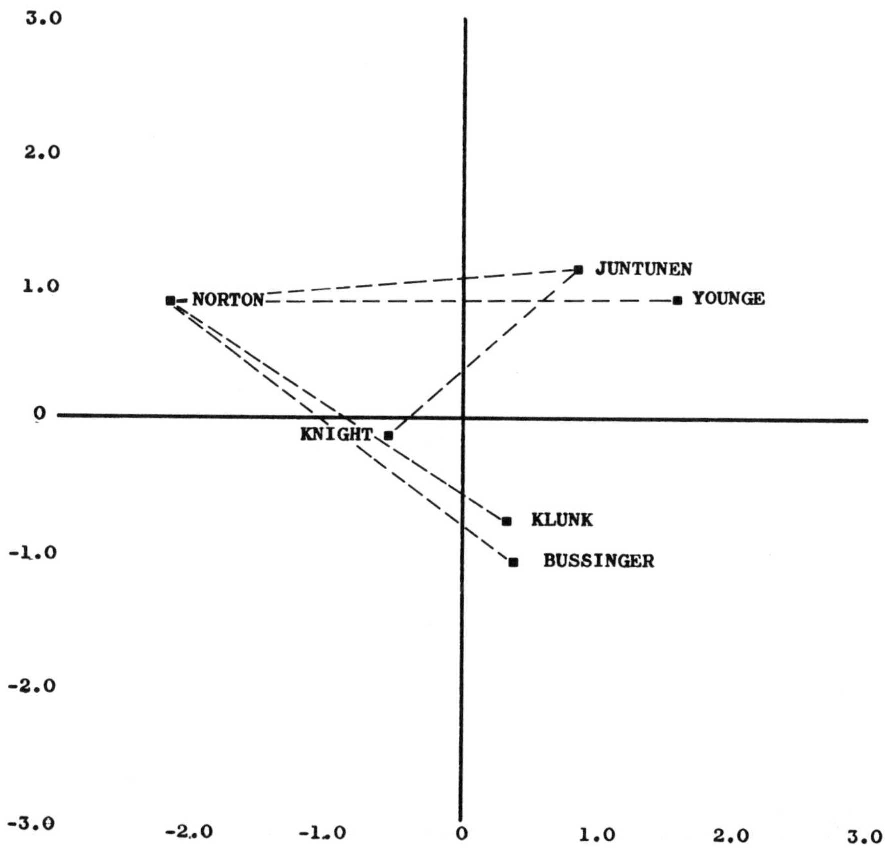

FIG. 7. Canonical Coefficients of 11 Cranial Indices.

vault variables, is very marked. The only difference in terms of significance involves the Knight-Younge and Klunk-Younge relationships, both of which are significantly different in terms of vault variables, but not in terms of cranial indices. The use of these cranial indices thus results in little or no additional information.

The 11 indices, in order of decreasing value in discrimination, are the following: height-length, orbital, gnathic, height-breadth, cranial module, upper facial, fronto-parietal, nasal, cranial, zygo-frontal and cranio-facial. Thus of the first five indices, three involve cranial height, which is an important discriminating variable in the other analyses.

EIGHTEEN POST-CRANIAL VARIABLES (FIG. 8)

Figure 8 illustrates the relationships based on 18 post-cranial variables and 5 skeletal series. In this analysis, the Steuben series (Illinois Hopewell) was added, while the Bussinger and Younge series were removed because of inadequate sample sizes. Steuben does not appear in the analyses based on cranial variables for the same reason.

The distances in Figure 8 are great, but none of the differences are significant. The isolation of the Juntunen series conforms well to the geographical and/or temporal isolation of the Juntunen site from the others, and the small distance between

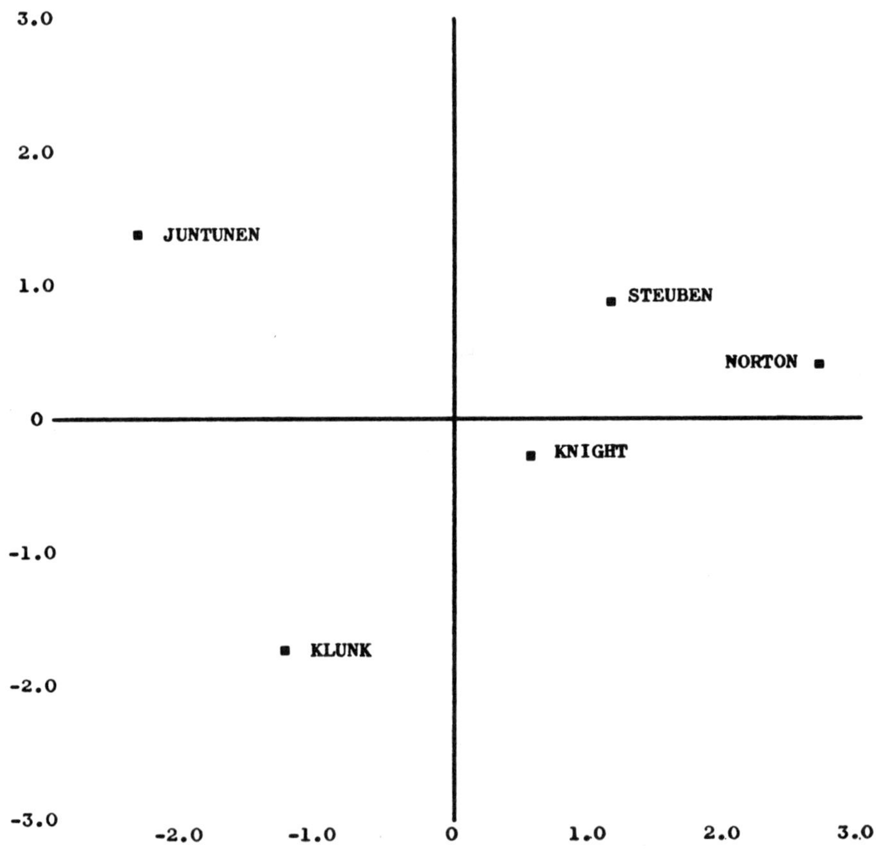

FIG. 8. Canonical Coefficients of 18 Post-Cranial Variables.

Norton and Steuben also parallels the cultural relatedness between these two series. Norton is also closer to Knight than it is to Klunk, a relationship which is observed in the previous analyses as well. The first six variables (FA'-P'; TA-P; HA-P; HHD; HM-L; FM-L), which account for most of the discrimination, are all measurements of widths as opposed to lengths. Since stature estimates are based on long bone lengths, and lengths were not of discriminatory value, and since long bone widths did not produce significant differences, it would follow that there are no significant differences in stature among these five series, irrespective of marked environmental and dietary differences.

Table 11 lists the stature estimates for 7 of the skeletal series used in this study. The estimates are based on the formulae of Genoves (1967) for Mesoamerican Indians, using femoral length as the estimator. In general, Genoves' estimates are shorter than those based on the formulae derived from Mongoloids and Mexicans by Trotter and Gleser (1958). Given a femoral length of 44.0 cm., the Genoves estimate is 163.5 cm., while Trotter and Gleser's formulae yield an estimate of 167.2 cm. for Mongoloids and 166.0 for Mexicans. While the estimates are thus different, the Genoves estimate is within a standard deviation of the Trotter and Gleser estimate. Furthermore, the identification of trends in stature is more meaningful than stature for stature's sake, especially when the amount of error is taken into account.

What is readily apparent from Table 11 is that there are no outstanding differences in stature, the maximum difference being 2.1 inches among the male samples. There is, however, an indication of a trend in increasing stature from south to north. The four northern or Michigan series, Norton, Bussinger, Juntunen and Backlund, all have mean stature estimates which exceed those of the Illinois series. While an increase in stature through time may be suggested in the comparison of Klunk (163.5 cm.) and Knight (165.8 cm.), data from Michigan fail to support this increase, as the Norton series is somewhat taller than two of the Late Woodland series. The small sample sizes, however, make any such statement concerning stature highly questionable. In general the female stature estimates parallel the males. The same trend is evident among the females, although the sample sizes are even smaller.

TABLE 11

STATURE ESTIMATION

Series	N	Range (cm.)	Mean	
BACKLUND				
Males	5	165.0 - 176.0	169.0	(66.5 in.)
Females	1	-	156.0	(61.4 in.)
NORTON				
Males	4	165.0 - 172.0	168.6	(66.4 in.)
Females	1	-	164.0	(64.6 in.)
BUSSINGER				
Males	5	163.0 - 172.0	167.7	(66.0 in.)
Females	2	162.0 - 163.5	162.8	(64.1 in.)
JUNTUNEN				
Males	15	159.0 - 182.0	167.2	(65.8 in.)
Females	10	154.5 - 167.0	159.5	(62.8 in.)
KNIGHT				
Males	16	151.0 - 174.0	165.8	(65.3 in.)
Females	9	151.0 - 164.0	156.5	(61.6 in.)
KLUNK				
Males	11	152.0 - 171.5	163.5	(64.4 in.)
Females	6	149.5 - 163.5	156.8	(61.7 in.)
STEUBEN				
Males	7	163.5 - 167.5	165.3	(65.1 in.)
Females	6	149.0 - 163.0	156.9	(61.8 in.)

EIGHT CRANIO-FACIAL VARIABLES (FIG. 9)

For this analysis, the four vault variables (H, B, L, BP) and four facial variables having the highest discriminatory values were employed. In addition to the original six skeletal series used in the previous analyses, the smaller Illinois Hopewell series, Snyders and Frederick, were included. A comparative series from the eastern Ontario site of Serpent Mounds (Anderson, 1968) was also included (Fig. 9).

The relationships between the six primary series are very similar to those seen in Figures 4 and 7 (vault variables and cranial indices, respectively), in that Norton is isolated and the Juntunen and Younge series are grouped, as are Knight, Klunk and Bussinger. Figure 9 also indicates the unrelatedness of the

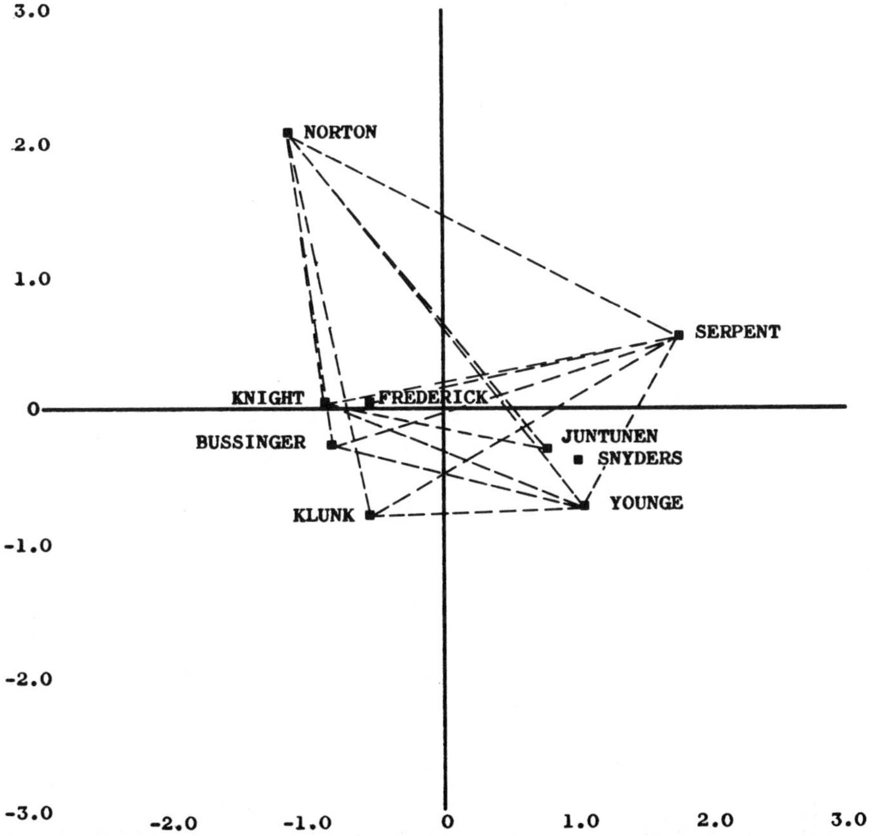

FIG. 9. Canonical Coefficients of 8 Cranio-Facial Variables.

Serpent Mounds series, which is significantly different from all other series except Juntunen and Snyders. The lack of significance involving the Snyders and Frederick series is due to the very small sample sizes (4 and 5 crania, respectively). The Frederick series, while significantly different from only Serpent Mounds, falls within the grouping containing the other Illinois series, Klunk and Knight. Archaeologically, the Snyders series should also be in this group, but is instead associated with the Juntunen-Younge group. The isolation of the Norton series in this analysis, as well as in the previous ones, is due primarily to an increased basion-bregma height and a decreased orbital height, relative to the other series. The first four variables chosen by the discriminant analysis were H, OH, B and AW.

NINE FACIAL VARIABLES (FIG. 10)

The 9 facial variables employed in this analysis are those used previously (Fig. 5), plus BN and BP, neither of which contribute significantly to the discrimination. Seven skeletal series taken from the literature are included in this analysis, in addition to 5 of the original 6 series. The inclusion of the series from the literature (indicated by open squares in Fig. 10) is accomplished by treating each population as an individual, this individual having as measurements the mean values for the population. Thus with 7 such populations, a single population of 7 individuals is designated for the purpose of plotting the canonical

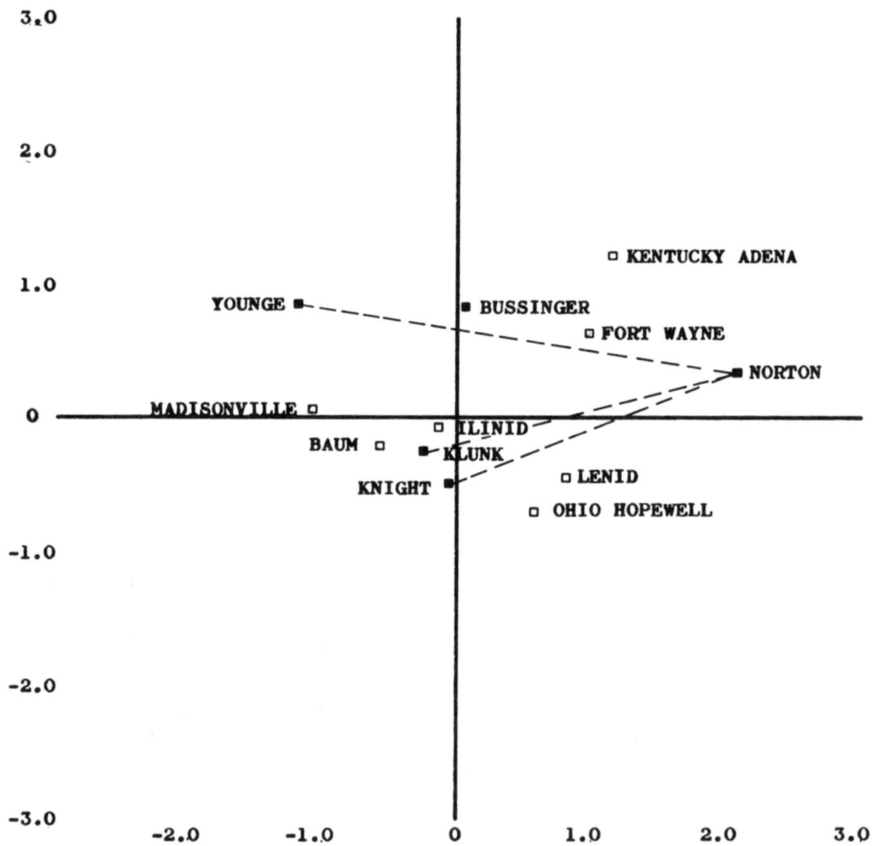

FIG. 10. Canonical Coefficients of 9 Facial Variables.

coefficients. The mean coordinates for this hypothetical population are ignored, and only the positions of the 7 "individuals" are recorded. This method precludes the calculation of F-values, so no significance can be established. By interpolation, however, the dashed lines of significance in Figure 10 can be used as a guide to the significance of the populations taken from the literature, to the extent that the distances correspond to significance.

In Figure 10, for example, the Norton series would appear to be significantly different from the Madisonville and Baum series,[1] but not from Fort Wayne, Lenid, Kentucky Adena or Ohio Hopewell. The position of the Ilinid series relative to Norton is questionable in terms of significance. Since the relationships among the 5 original series—Norton, Knight, Klunk, Younge and Bussinger—are basically unchanged from what they were in Figure 5, it is the position of the other 7 populations that is of interest here. The proximity of the Bussinger and Fort Wayne series conforms to the archaeological relationships between the two (Halsey, 1968), and the Mississippian association of the Baum and Madisonville series should place them closer to the southern Illinois groups than to the Michigan groups. The position of the Norton series is not clarified by this analysis, however, as it is similarly close to Kentucky Adena, Ohio Hopewell, Fort Wayne and Neumann's Lenid series. The Lenid series, incidentally, is quite close to the Ilinid series. The Ilinid variety reportedly developed from the Lenid variety (Neumann, 1960), the differentiation presumably complete enough to warrant the establishment of two distinct varieties.

ELEVEN CRANIO-FACIAL VARIABLES (FIG. 11)

The variables used in this last analysis were chosen to incorporate several series from the literature. In addition to the Ilinid, Lenid and Fort Wayne series, an Ohio Hopewell series of 13 males from the Turner site in southern Ohio (Hooton, 1922) is included, and the Backlund, Serpent Mounds, Frederick and Snyders series are added to the original 6 series used in the earlier analyses.

What is perhaps somewhat too obvious from the number of dashed lines in Figure 11 is that there are a great many significant

[1] Madisonville and Baum are Mississippian sites of the Fort Ancient culture in southern Ohio with a temporal span of A.D. 1000 to 1650 (Griffin, 1943; Robbins, 1968). Fort Wayne is a Late Woodland site near Detroit.

differences involved in the relationships depicted here. On closer inspection however, it is in reality just 3 of the 10 series which are significantly different from most of the others. The Norton series remains significantly different from all but 2 of the series—Snyders and Knight—excluding those series taken from the literature, denoted by open squares in Figure 11. The Serpent Mounds series, as in Figure 9, is different from all but the Snyders and Juntunen series, although the comments concerning the small sample size of the Snyders series made above apply here as well. Finally, the Backlund series is significantly different from all of the other 9 series, as was predicted on the basis of visual comparisons. Regarding the accuracy of classification, only the Backlund

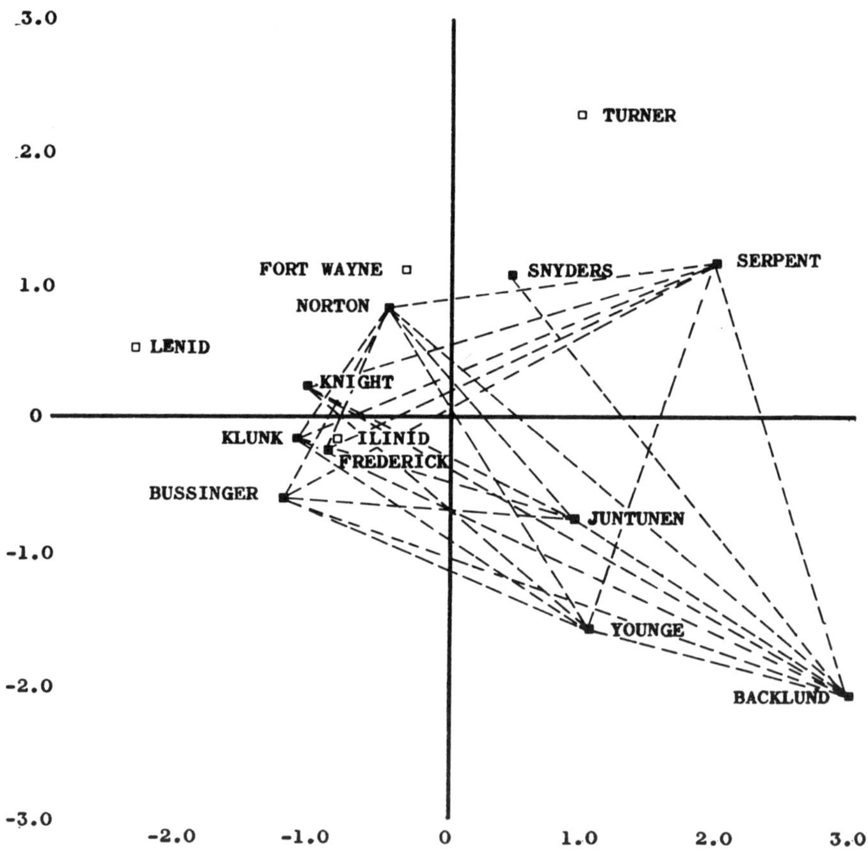

FIG. 11. Canonical Coefficients of 11 Cranio-Facial Variables.

series was classified correctly, despite the small sample size of 4 crania.

In terms of larger groupings of the various series, Figure 11 is quite similar to several of the previous analyses, in that the Juntunen—Younge and the Knight-Klunk-Frederick-Bussinger constellations are again evident. The Norton series is somewhat closer to this last major group than in previous runs, and shows more affinity to the Illinois based series than it does to those from Michigan, with the exception of the Fort Wayne series. This similarity between Norton and Fort Wayne may be of some significance, considering the intermediate temporal position of the Fort Wayne series relative to Norton on the one hand, and Juntunen and Younge on the other. Despite the significant differences, the proximity of the Backlund series to Juntunen and Younge in Figure 11, compared to the Illinois, Ohio or Ontario series, is at least reasonable.

The closeness of Snyders to Norton would also be reasonable considering the archaeological similarities, but the Snyders-Serpent Mounds similarity is inexplicable in these terms. It is interesting to note the positions of the Lenid and Ilinid series in relation to the others, as the Ilinid series falls within a series cluster consisting of three of the Illinois series and the Bussinger series, and is quite close to Norton. There does not appear to be a close relationship between the Ilinids and the other Michigan Late Woodland groups or Serpent Mounds. The Lenid series is even further removed from Juntunen, Younge, Backlund and Serpent Mounds, but fairly close to the Illinois cluster and the Ilinid series. The Ohio Hopewellian series from the Turner site is isolated from all of the other series, the closest similarity being with an Illinois Middle Woodland series, Snyders, on the one hand, and an Ontario Middle Woodland group, Serpent Mounds, on the other.

In general, several relationships are repeatedly suggested in the discriminant analyses. There is a marked tendency for the Illinois groups from the Klunk, Knight and Frederick sites to cluster, with the Bussinger series being included when the analysis is based at least partially on vault variables. In a similar fashion, the Juntunen and Younge series show a marked affinity, especially in terms of vault variables. The Norton series is quite consistently isolated from both of these clusters, although somewhat closer to the Illinois groups, particularly the Knight series, again in terms of vault variables. In terms of facial variables, the Norton orientation is more in the direction of the Michigan Late Woodland series.

PROFILE PATTERN ANALYSIS

The various relationships mentioned in the proceeding section of this chapter are based upon comparisons of size, not shape; Figures 12 and 13 illustrate quite well these size and shape differences. Figure 12, which compares a Backlund male

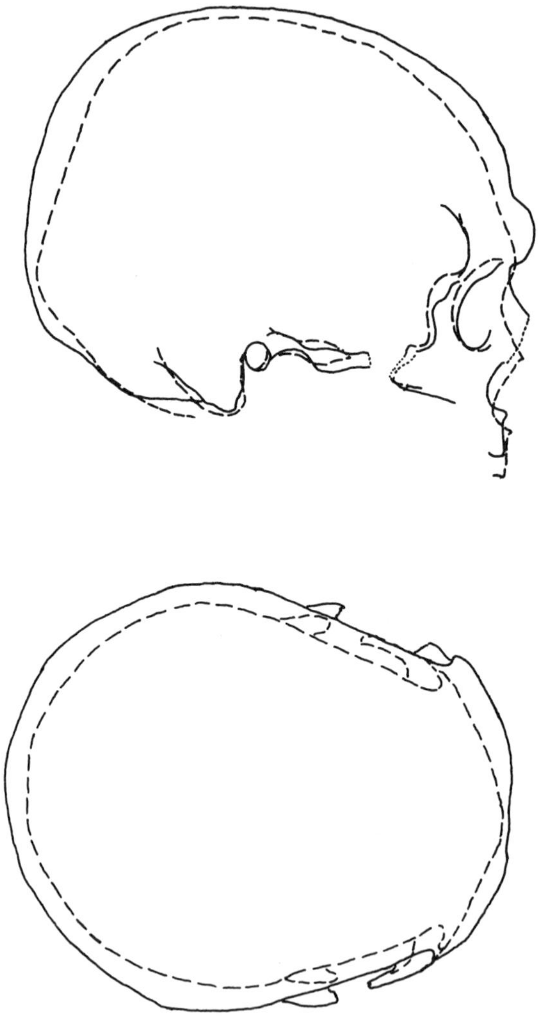

FIG. 12. Cranial Outlines: Lateral and Dorsal Views (x-1/2). (Solid line = Backlund male; dashed line = Norton male)

with one from the Norton Mounds, illustrates differences in both size and shape. The Backlund skull is clearly of a greater size than the Norton skull, but the shapes of the two skulls are also dissimilar. The effect of deformation is also readily apparent in the outline of the Norton skull. Figure 13, illustrating two males from the same feature of the Juntunen site, shows primarily differences in size.

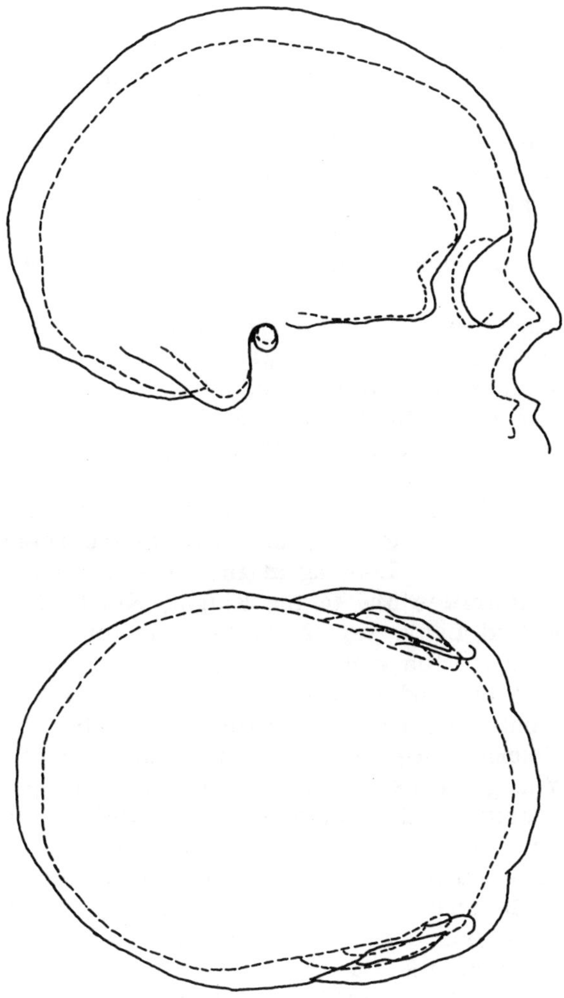

FIG. 13. Cranial Outlines: Lateral and Dorsal Views (x-1/2).
(Solid line = Juntunen, 41244; dashed line = Juntunen, 41241)

In order to evaluate the relationships based on shape comparisons, the means for the male cranio-facial and mandibular variables were converted to T-scores, as discussed in Chapter I. Correlation coefficients for the T-scores of the several variables in two groups were then calculated, a positive correlation coefficient (r_T) indicating similarity. The results of this analysis, in terms of r_T, are summarized in Table 12. The correlation coefficients, whether positive or negative, are low, and most are not significant. This is most likely due to the small size of the general population with which each series was compared for calculation of the T-scores. Due to this lack of significance, the r_T values can only be considered as indicators of possible similarities or differences, or of trends in these directions. Increasing the size of the base population would have the effect of increasing the value of r_T, but it most likely would not effect the sign.

Figures 14 through 32 illustrate the profile patterns for various combinations of series. These patterns provide a visual indication of the overall similarities between two series, and are very useful in illustrating where the differences or similarities lie, in terms of the variables involved. The figures illustrate 19 of the 91 profile patterns, with an emphasis on the Norton series, as its relationships are of primary importance in this study.

Returning to Table 12, the overall impression from the r_T values is that the profile analysis parallels the results of the discriminant analysis. Looking at the Norton series, for example, the similarities are to the Knight, Klunk, Frederick, Turner, Ilinid and Lenid series, at least in terms of positive r_T values. The Norton series is different from the various Michigan Late Woodland series, as well as from the Snyders series. The only significant r_T value for Norton is that between Norton and Younge; most of the discriminant analyses also show Norton and Younge to be the most dissimilar groups.

The similarity of the Knight-Klunk-Frederick cluster suggested from the discriminant analyses is again evident here, as is the Juntunen-Younge relationship. Juntunen also appears similar to Serpent Mounds, as indicated in Figures 9 and 11 of the discriminant analysis section. While showing some similarity to the Klunk series, the Bussinger crania are not similar to Knight, Norton or Frederick as in the discriminant analyses. Nor is the Bussinger series similar to Juntunen, and shows only a slight similarity to Younge, while being most similar to the Fort Wayne series. The Bussinger-Fort Wayne similarity was

TABLE 12

T-SCORE CORRELATION COEFFICIENTS

	Knight	Klunk	Frederick	Snyders	Bussinger	Fort Wayne	Serpent	Juntunen	Younge	Turner	Backlund	Ilinid	Lenid
Norton	.288	.015	.054	-.296	-.297	-.087	-.085	-.101	-.541*	.223	-.117	.066	.231
Knight	-	.366*	.497*	-.269	-.252	-.118	-.053	-.381*	-.647*	.352	-.397*	.159	.094
Klunk	-	-	.205	-.505*	.113	.417	-.359	-.359	-.444*	.323	-.776*	.247	.296
Frederick	-	-	-	.125	-.192	-.354	-.120	-.573*	-.279	.197	-.134	-.080	-.410
Snyders	-	-	-	-	-.373*	.014	.306	.245	.460*	-.204	.467*	-.106	.106
Bussinger	-	-	-	-	-	.485	-.191	-.084	.023	.011	-.313	-.232	-.137
Fort Wayne	-	-	-	-	-	-	-.447	-.001	-.110	.035	-.265	-.106	.142
Serpent	-	-	-	-	-	-	-	.342	.239	.318	.225	.405	.598*
Juntunen	-	-	-	-	-	-	-	-	.246	-.179	.305	-.195	.187
Younge	-	-	-	-	-	-	-	-	-	-.391	.555*	.122	.019
Turner	-	-	-	-	-	-	-	-	-	-	-.290	.326	.370
Backlund	-	-	-	-	-	-	-	-	-	-	-	-.198	-.351
Ilinid	-	-	-	-	-	-	-	-	-	-	-	-	.571*

*P = .05

first suggested in Figure 10, based on the discriminant analysis of facial variables.

The Backlund series remains different from many of the other series, although it is quite clear from Table 12 that some of the differences of the discriminant analysis section noted in Figure 11 are due to size. When shape is considered, Backlund shows some similarity to the Serpent Mounds and Juntunen series, and especially to the Snyders and Younge series. That the Backlund series appears to be related to neither the Ilinid nor Lenid series is not too surprising, since the same is true for the Frederick and Bussinger series. On the other hand, six of the series have positive correlations with both the Ilinid and Lenid series, and these two series are themselves significantly correlated (r_T = .571).

The relationships implied by the r_T values in Table 12 are based on the total number of variables recorded, and thus do not reflect differences or similarities within particular regions of the skull, except as these regions influence the final r_T value. Hence a great difference in a single variable can mask similarities in several other variables, or vice versa. The use of profile patterns provides the solution to this problem, however, as the relationship between two series is illustrated for each variable.

NORTON-KNIGHT

Figure 14 illustrates the profile pattern for the Norton-Knight comparison. There is an overall similarity between the two series, and yet some rather marked differences. The value of r_T is increased positively when the T-scores of a variable fall on the same side of the T = 50 line for both series, negatively if the T-scores are on opposite sides; a T-score of 50.0 for a variable in either series neither increases nor decreases the value of r_T. Figure 14 illustrates that the vault variables are the major contributors to the positive r_T value. In particular, it is obvious that the two series are similar in terms of the minimum frontal diameter (MF), basion-bregma height (H) and auricular height (AH). While the facial region is basically different, similarities do exist in nasal width (NW) and in the length and width of the palate (AL, AW). The marked difference in orbital width (OW) does not reduce the positive value of r_T, however, since the T-score for the Knight series is 50.0. The mandibular variables (SH, BL, BGW, BCW, RH and RW) are in

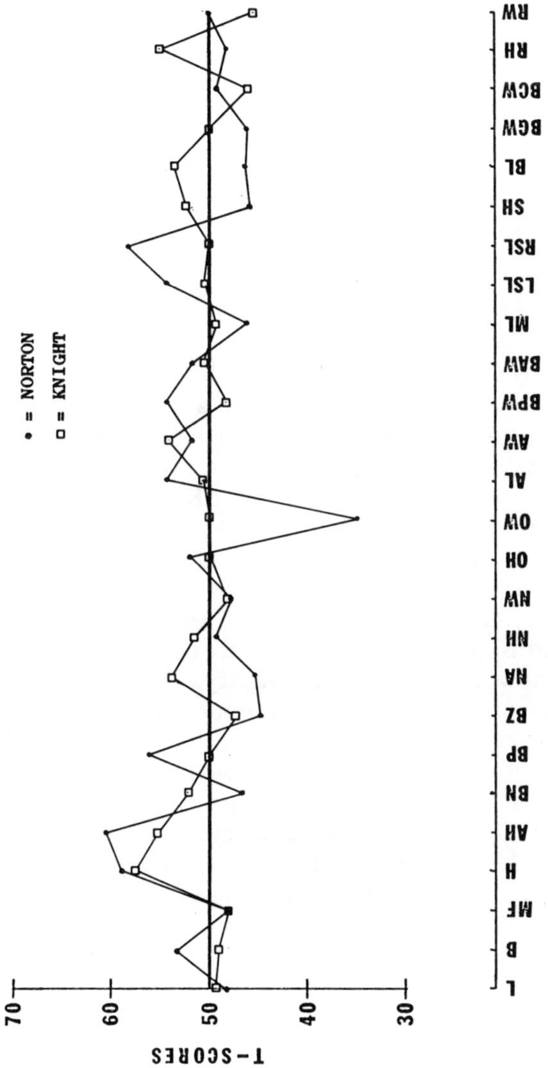

FIG. 14. Norton-Knight Profile Pattern (r_T = .228).

general different in the two series, and tend to depress the positive r_T value.

The effects of bifronto-occipital deformation, common in a slight to moderate degree among the Norton crania and present in a few of the Knight crania, are obvious in Figure 14, especially in terms of the elevated cranial heights. To a lesser extent the reduced minimum frontal diameter might also be a result of the deformation, although a relatively great height and narrow frontal have been seen as characteristic of undeformed Hopewellian skulls as well (Stewart, 1943). The deformation might also be responsible for the shorter maximum length, although the difference from the total mean is very slight in the Norton and Knight series.

NORTON-KLUNK

Figure 15 illustrates the Norton-Klunk profile pattern, in which $r_T = .015$. There thus does not appear to be any meaningful similarity between these two Hopewellian series. Considering the vault variables, it is clear that the similarities are again mostly in terms of cranial height (H, AH) and minimum frontal diameter. As was the case in the Norton-Knight comparison (Fig. 14), there is also substantial similarity in bizygomatic breadth (BZ). Although the Norton and Klunk series are thus similar in terms of total facial width, the other width variables, maximum breadth (B), biporionic width (BPW) and biasterionic width (BAW) show marked dissimilarity.

In the facial region, there is some similarity in three of the variables, nasal height (NH), nasal width (NW) and palate width (AW). These similarities are considerably overshadowed by the differences in the other facial variables, notably orbital width (OW), since the fact that Klunk is above the mean T-score and Norton is far below it results in a large negative contribution to r_T. In the mandibular region, the large difference in symphysis height (SH) outweighs the smaller similarities in BL, BGW and BCW, thus the total contribution from the mandible is negative.

NORTON-JUNTUNEN

The profile patterns of the Norton and Juntunen series are shown in Figure 16. There are obvious differences in the vault variables, especially in the cranial heights and minimum frontal

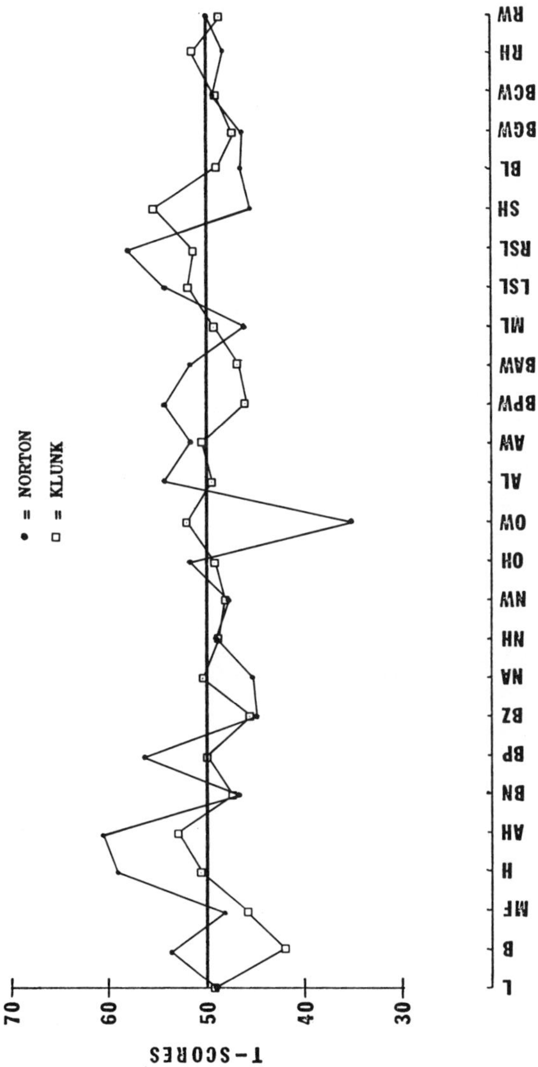

FIG. 15. Norton-Klunk Profile Pattern (r_T = .015).

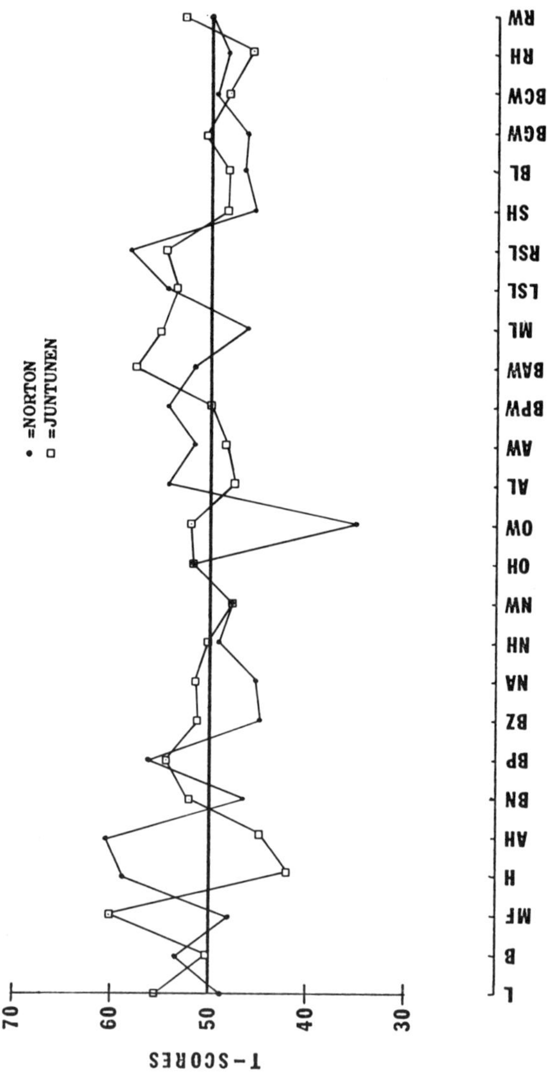

FIG. 16. Norton-Juntunen Profile Pattern (r_T = -.101).

diameter, exactly those variables which were responsible for much of the Norton-Knight and Norton-Klunk similarities. There is also an opposite relationship involving breadth variables as compared to the Norton-Klunk pattern. While the bizygomatic diameter results in a negative contribution in the present analysis, there are similarities in maximum breadth and biasterionic width.

With the exception of nasal width, the facial variables also contribute to the negative r_T. Since Figure 5 of the discriminant analyses indicated that Norton and Juntunen were not significantly different in terms of the facial variables, the similarities between the two series are thus features of size but not shape. Among the mandibular variables, only bigonial width (BGW) is negative, the two series being otherwise similar in terms of the mandibular variables.

NORTON-YOUNGE

The Norton-Younge profile pattern, illustrated in Figure 17, is similar to the Norton-Juntunen pattern, with the differences being more extreme in the present case. Again there are the marked dissimilarities in the height, minimum frontal and bizgomatic variables, and a similarity in two of the three vault breadth variables (B and BPW).

Differences in the facial variables seen in the Norton-Juntunen comparison are more strongly emphasized between Norton and Younge. Although there is some similarity in the nasal variables, the orbital and palate variables show large differences. Three of the mandibular variables contribute negatively to the correlation (BGW, BCW and RH), two positively (SH and BL) while RW contributes nothing. The negative contributions are, moreover, considerably larger than the positive.

The relatively high negative correlation coefficient for the two patterns (r_T = -.541) is significant at the .05 level. The magnitude of this difference is understandable considering that 20 of the 26 variables show a difference which results in either a negative correlation, or none at all. It is not only difference in variable value that causes the large negative value of r_T, but that the differences are large when present. The overall dissimilarity of the Norton and Younge series was also obvious in most of the discriminant analyses, in which the distance between Norton and Younge is generally the greatest of any of the

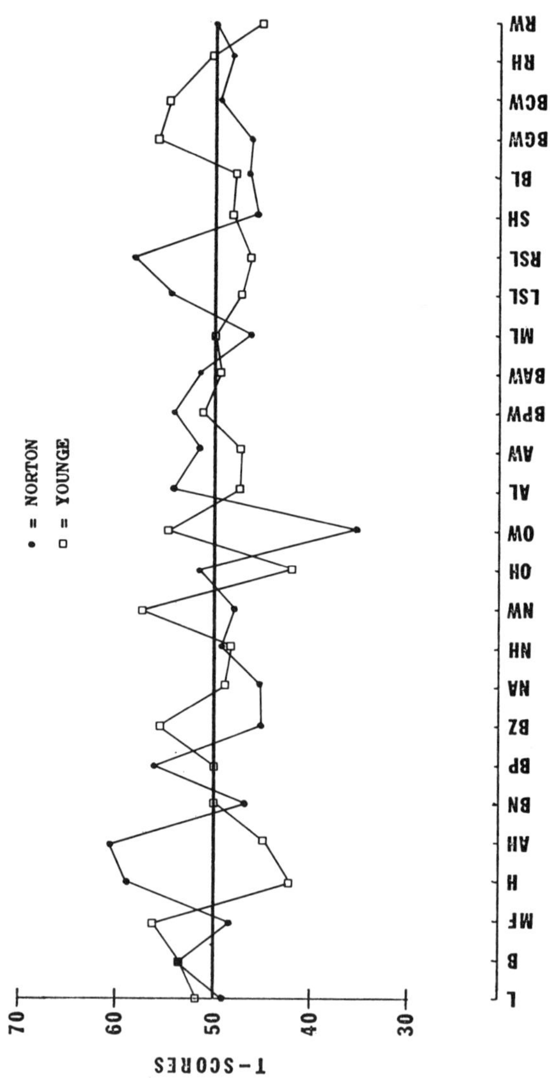

FIG. 17. Norton-Younge Profile Pattern (r_T = -.541).

comparisons. With the exception of the analysis based on mandibular variables (Fig. 6), the Norton-Younge difference is always significant at the .01 level.

NORTON-BUSSINGER

Figure 18 illustrates the profile patterns of the Norton and Bussinger series. In the vault variables there are some obvious differences, particularly in the cranial height variables, as the Bussinger series is definitely low-vaulted. Unlike the Juntunen and Younge series, Bussinger is characterized by a narrow minimum frontal diameter, and is thus similar to Norton in this respect. The only other vault similarities involve maximum and minimum length (L, ML) and bizygomatic diameter. The Norton-Bussinger relationship involving cranial breadths is similar to those observed in the Norton-Klunk comparison, and unlike the comparisons with the Late Woodland sites, Juntunen and Younge. Figure 18 thus indicates that Norton and Bussinger are dissimilar in maximum breadth, biporionic width and biasterionic width, but similar in bizygomatic breadth.

The facial region is essentially similar in the two series, with the exception of the palate (AW, AL). It should be recalled that in the discriminant analysis using 7 facial variables (Fig. 5) the difference between Norton and Bussinger was not significant. Three of the 6 mandibular variables indicate a similarity (SH, BGW and RH), 2 contribute negatively to r_T (BL and BCW) and the contribution of ramus width is zero.

NORTON-TURNER

The correlation coefficient of the profile patterns of these 2 Hopewellian groups is based upon 18 variables, instead of the usual 26 (Fig. 19), as several of the variables used in this study were not included in Hooton's report. The Turner crania utilized here are supposedly undeformed, but the narrow minimum frontal and increased height are evident in this series, as they were in the Knight and Klunk series. There is, however, no evidence of the shortened cranial length as seen in the various series in which deformation is present. The inverse relationship between cranial and facial breadths is again evident in these two series. The Norton series, with its relatively wide interparietal distance and narrow facial width (B and BZ) would

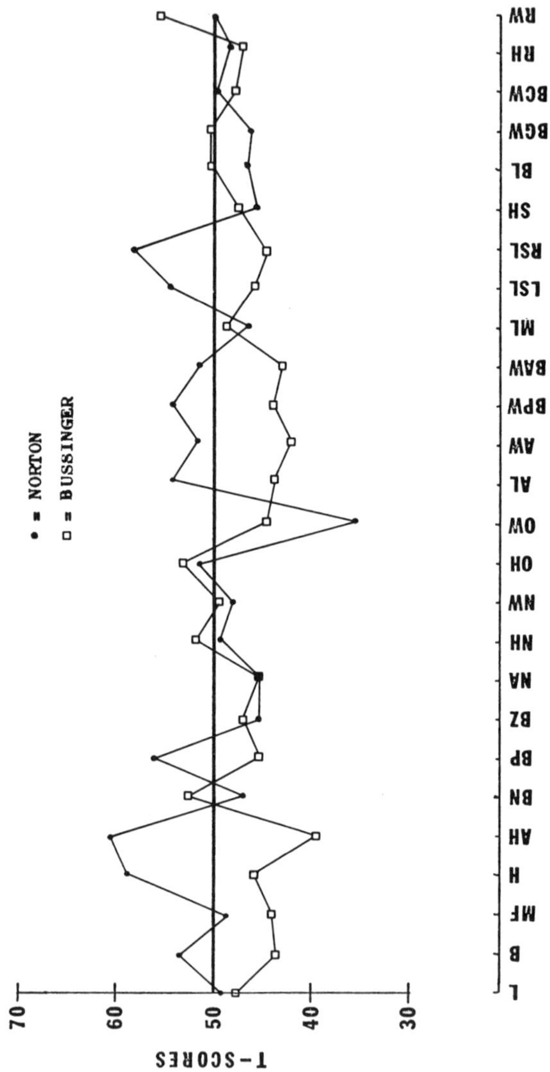

FIG. 18. Norton-Bussinger Profile Pattern (r_T = -.297).

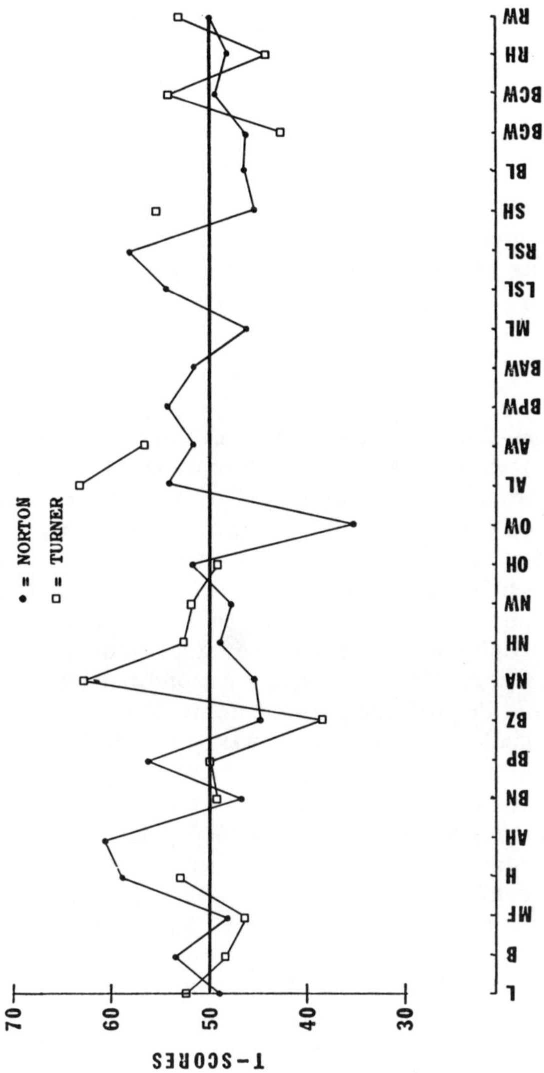

FIG. 19. Norton-Turner Profile Pattern (r_T = .223).

appear to be the determining factor in these width relationships, as the profile patterns which do not include the Norton group (Figs. 23-32) do not exhibit this phenomenon.

In the facial region, similarities are confined to the lower face, namely the palate, while the upper facial area exhibits some marked differences in terms of upper facial height (NA), nasal length and width and orbital height. Orbital width could not be used because it could not be determined whether maxillo-frontale or dacyron was used in the measurement of the Turner series.

The mandibular variables show two distinct differences, in symphysis height and bicondylar width, and equally distinct similarities in bigonial width and ramus height. Ramus width, as in all comparisons involving the Norton series, does not contribute to r_T.

NORTON-LENID

The Norton-Lenid profile pattern, illustrated in Figure 20, is based on 18 variables, the maximum number of variables similar to mine that are listed by Robbins (1968). In the vault region, similarity is restricted to three variables, BN, BP and BZ. The major vault dimensions of length, breadth and height account for negative contributions to r_T. The narrow frontal diameter and high vault of the Norton series and those from Illinois are not evident among the Lenid crania.

The facial region also exhibits a combination of similarities and differences, the differences centering around variables of facial height, such as nasion-alveolar point (NA), nasal height and orbital height. There is similarity in nasal and orbital widths, and in palate length. The similarity in orbital width and palate length accounts for a large portion of the positive contribution to r_T, as the T-scores for these variables are quite far removed from the mean in both series. The mandibular variables also increase r_T positively, as three of the four variables are similar in their deviation from the mean T-score.

While the T-scores of the Norton and Lenid series are positively correlated, the general impression from Figure 20 is that the two series are not particularly similar, especially in terms of vault shape. Excluding the mandible, the two series are similar in only 6 of 14 variables.

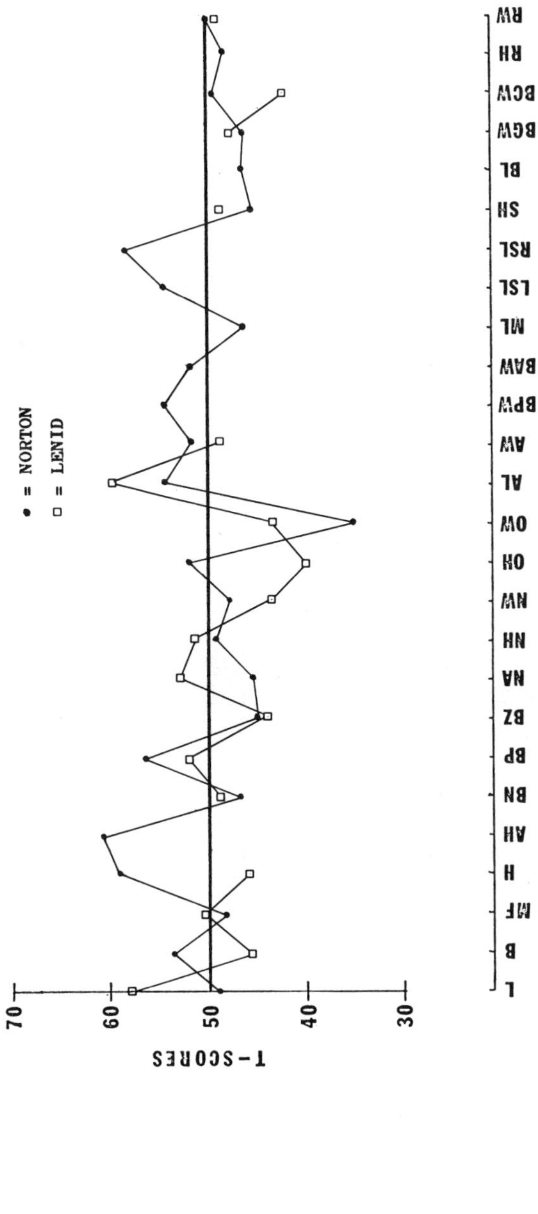

FIG. 20. Norton-Lenid Profile Pattern (r_T = .231).

NORTON-ILINID

The correlation coefficient of the Norton-Ilinid profile pattern (r_T = .066) suggests little if any relationship between these two series. As illustrated in Figure 21, similarities in the cranial vaults are found in basion-bregma height, basion-prosthion length (BP) and bizygomatic breadth, the remaining vault variables showing moderate dissimilarity.

The facial regions of the two series are more similar than the vault regions, as 4 of the 6 facial variables make positive contributions to the value of r_T. There is a slight dissimilarity in nasal height between the Norton and Ilinid series, and a more marked dissimilarity in orbital height. As in the Norton-Lenid comparison (Fig. 20), orbital width and palate length are major contributors to the positive correlation. In the mandibular region the contribution to r_T would be negative, due to the rather large difference in symphysis height, which would offset the similarities in bigonial and bicondylar width.

NORTON-SNYDERS

The Norton-Snyders comparison, depicted in Figure 22, is basically one of dissimilarity, as suggested by the negative correlation coefficient (r_T = -.296). Although the series are similar in 6 of the 11 vault variables, the differences in the remaining 5 variables, in terms of magnitude of deviation from the mean, are considerably greater than the similarities. Among the vault variables, the differences in basion-bregma and auricular height and bizygomatic diameter are the most obvious.

Of the 7 facial variables, 4 (NA, NW, AL, AW) result in positive contributions to r_T, and 3 are different. The magnitude of difference in orbital width is obvious, and is responsible for a large part of the negative correlation coefficient.

The differences in the vault region are basically similar to those encountered in the comparisons of Norton with Juntunen (Fig. 16) and Younge (Fig. 17). The Snyders site is thus fairly similar to these two Michigan series, as indicated by the positive r_T values in Table 11. The discriminant analysis based on 8 cranio-facial variables (Fig. 9) shows these relationships very clearly.

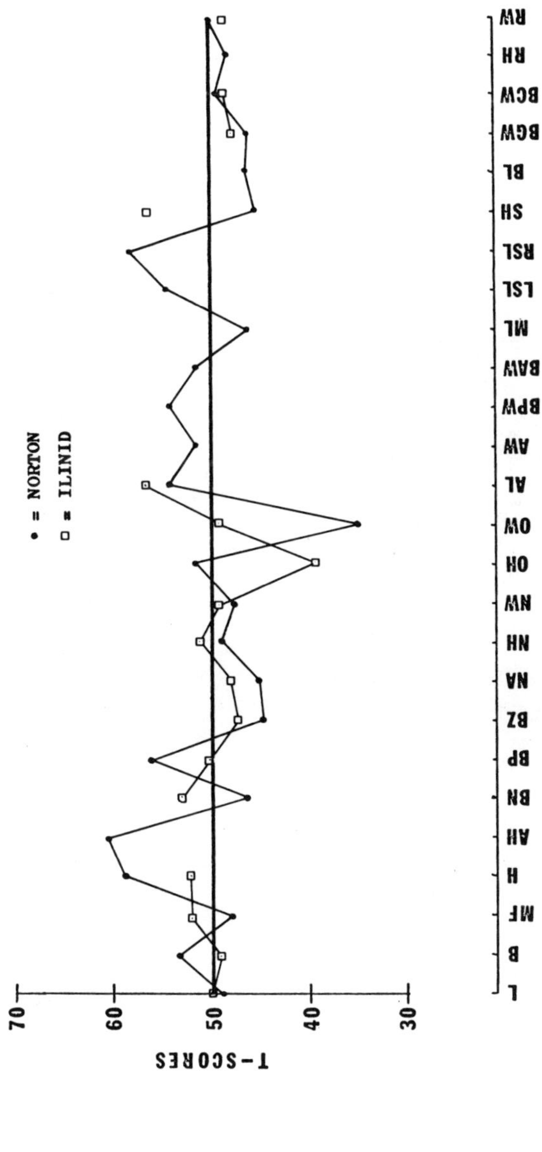

FIG. 21. Norton-Ilinid Profile Pattern (r_T = .066).

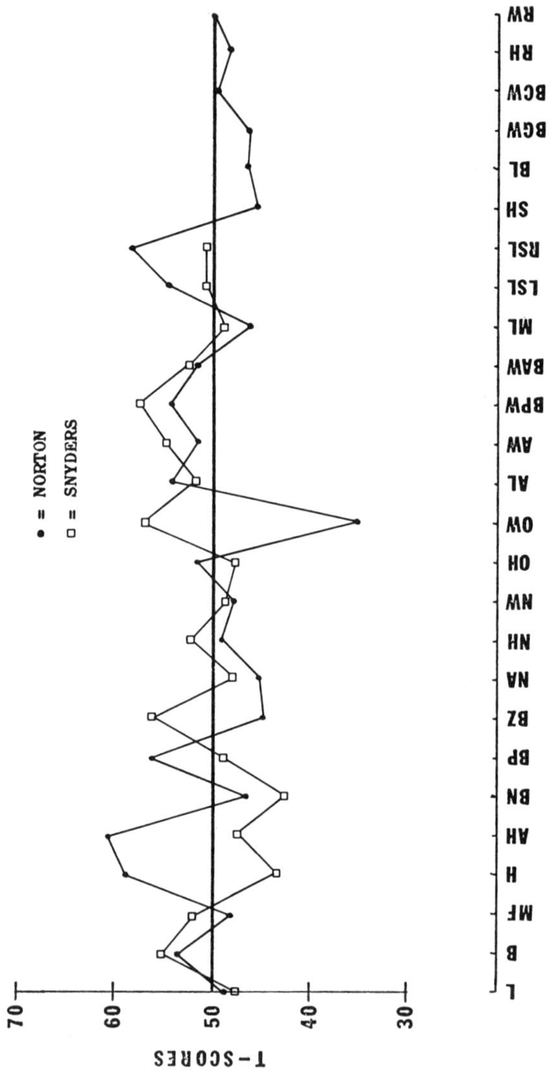

FIG. 22. Norton-Snyders Profile Pattern (r_T = -.296).

KNIGHT-KLUNK

All of the discriminant analyses suggest a close relationship between the Knight and Klunk series, and this relatedness is again indicated by the profile patterns shown in Figure 23, the correlation coefficient being positive and fairly high (r_T = .366). The two series are similar in 9 of 11 vault variables, with only basion-nasion (BN) and biasterionic width (BAW) contributing negatively.

In a similar fashion, only two of the facial variables (NH, AL) and two mandibular variables (SH, BL) detract from the positive correlation. The small amount of deviation of the variables from the mean T-score values evident in Figure 23 is due to the fact that these two series were the major contributors to the establishment of the mean. By using larger, more inclusive series to establish the means, the deviations within the Knight and Klunk series should be greater, and the correlation coefficient correspondingly higher.

These results indicate that there were no major changes in the physical type of Indian populations in the Calhoun County, Illinois area during the transition from Middle to Late Woodland. Neumann's postulated change from the Lenid to the Ilinid variety during Middle Woodland times (Neumann, 1960) would at first appear to have some support from the values of r_T in Table 12. The Knight-Ilinid r_T value is slightly greater than the Knight-Lenid value, and Klunk appears slightly more similar to Lenid than to Ilinid. Yet on closer inspection of Table 12, Knight and Klunk are seen to be more similar to each other than either is to Neumann's varieties. More importantly, the varieties themselves are much more similar to each other than they are to the populations from the various sites.

KNIGHT-JUNTUNEN

Figure 24 illustrates the Knight-Juntunen profile pattern, and in general confirms the negative correlation between the two series (r_T = -.381). Considering first the vault variables, only two—basion-nasion and biasterionic width—indicate a similarity between the series. These variables are precisely those which indicated the only *dissimilarity* between the vaults of the Knight and Klunk series in the previous analysis (Fig. 23). As in the

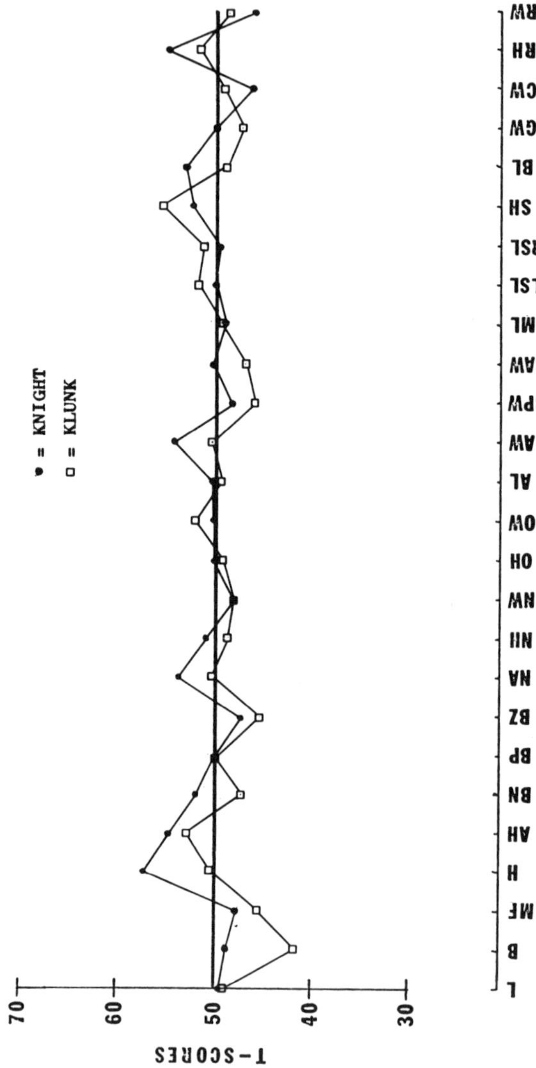

FIG. 23. Knight-Klunk Profile Pattern (r_T = .366).

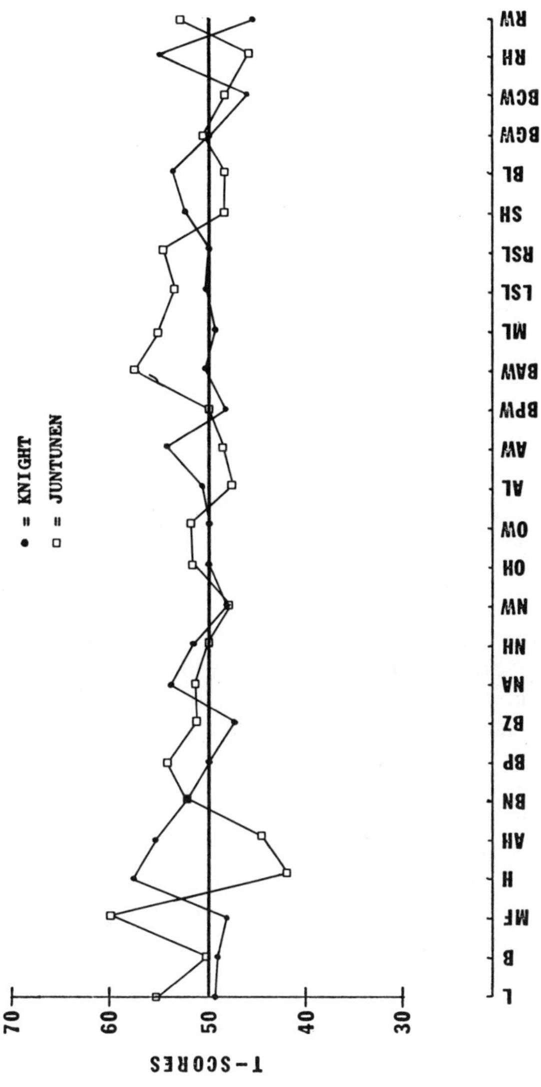

FIG. 24. Knight-Juntunen Profile Pattern (r_T = -.381).

comparisons involving the Norton series, minimum frontal diameter and cranial height variables are the most obvious areas of difference.

In the facial region there is an overall similarity between the two sites, with a zero contribution being made by three variables (NH, OH, OW). It is only the palate variables which increase the negative value of the correlation. These relationships based on shape agree very closely with those based on size, as Juntunen and Knight are significantly different in terms of vault variables (Fig. 4), but very close when facial variables are considered (Fig. 5).

The mandibular variables increase the negative correlation, for the most part. The two series differ in 4 variables (SH, BL, RH, RW), while only bicondylar width contributes positively to r_T. Figure 6, illustrating the results of the discriminant analysis based on mandibular variables, tends to reinforce the evidence of this mandibular difference.

KNIGHT-ILINID

The Knight-Ilinid profile pattern, based on 18 variables, is illustrated in Figure 25. The two series are generally similar in terms of the vault variables, as 4 of these 7 variables add to the positive correlation (r_T = .159), while only 1—minimum frontal diameter—has a negative correlation. The T-scores of the length, breadth, basion-nasion, basion-prosthion and bizygomatic diameter variables are nearly identical in the two series.

There is also a general similarity in facial variables, although the fairly large discrepancies in nasion-alveolar point length (NA) and palate width (AW) detract substantially from this similarity. The two series are likewise similar in three of the four mandibular variables.

The overall impression of the Knight-Ilinid relationship is one of greater similarity than that suggested by the correlation coefficient. This impression is intensified by the results of the discriminant analysis, as the two series are very close in Figures 10 and 11.

KLUNK-LENID

Figure 26 illustrates the Klunk-Lenid relationship, one which is fairly close as indicated by the moderately high and positive

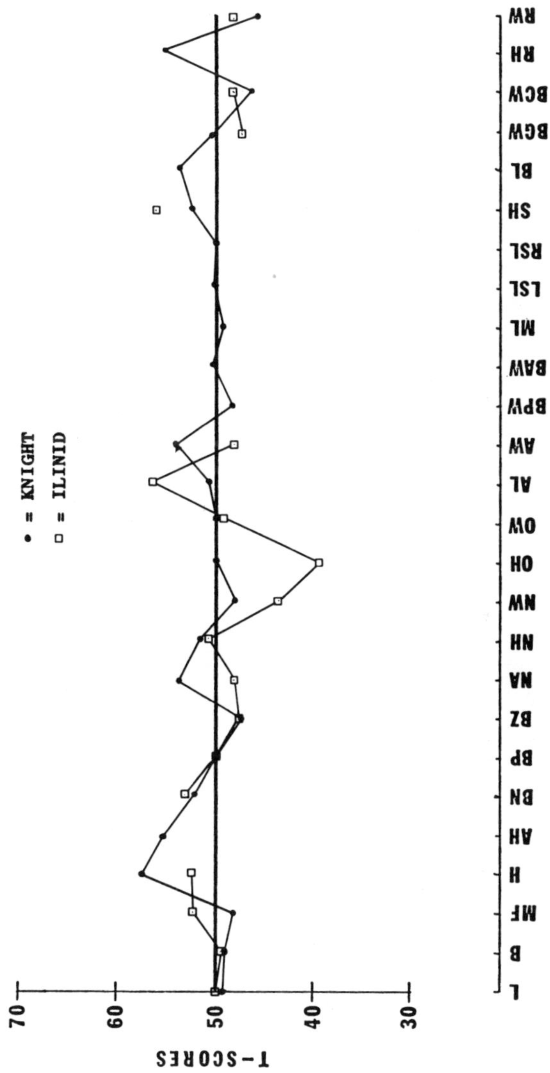

FIG. 25. Knight-Ilinid Profile Pattern (r_T = .159).

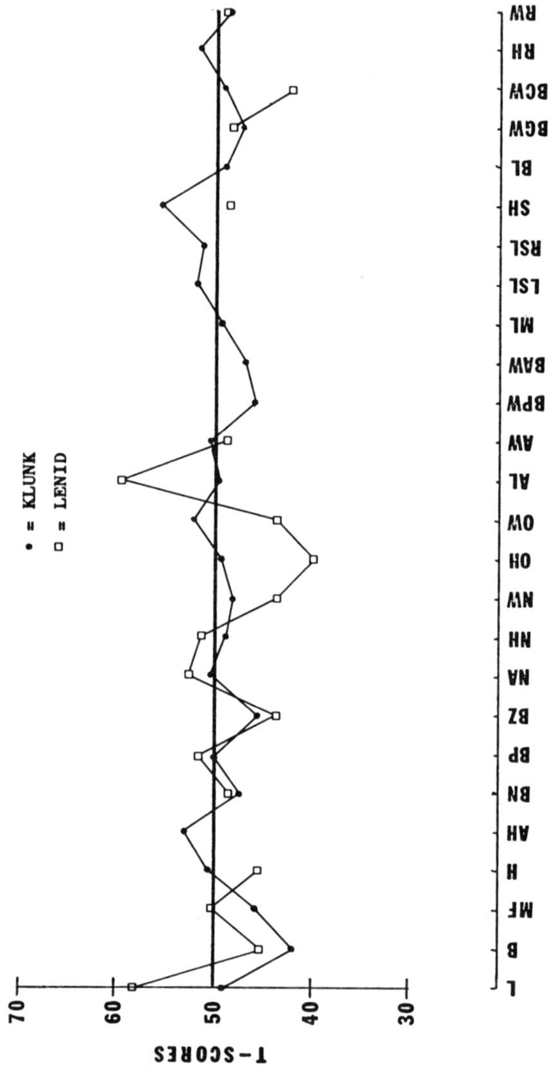

FIG. 26. Klunk-Lenid Profile Pattern (r_T = .296).

r_T value (.296), again based on 18 variables. Of the vault variables, dissimilarities are encountered in maximum length, minimum frontal diameter and basion-bregma height. Narrow skull breadth, as indicated by the low T-scores for maximum and bizygomatic breadth, is a source of similarity in the two series.

The facial region is basically dissimilar, although three of the variables, NA, NW and OH, are factors increasing the correlation coefficient. The mandible also contributes to the positive r_T, as 3 of the 4 variables deviate similarly from the mean in both series.

KLUNK-YOUNGE

The notable differences between the Klunk and Younge series indicated in the discriminant analyses are equally evident in terms of the profile analysis, illustrated in Figure 27. With the exception of basion-prosthion (BP) and biasterionic width, the vault variables show rather marked differences between the two series. This dissimilarity in vault measurements is evident in terms of size (Figs. 3 and 4) as well as shape (Fig. 27).

Four of the facial variables are similar, but the fact that the Klunk series varies but little from the overall mean results in a relatively small positive contribution to r_T. The significant negative value of r_T is further increased by the mandibular variables, as 4 of the 6 variables show varying degrees of difference.

Figure 27 is similar to Figure 24 (Knight-Juntunen), as would be expected since Knight and Klunk are unquestionably similar, and Juntunen and Younge show strong similarities, at least in terms of the vault. Once again, the results of the shape analysis have basically affirmed those obtained from the size analysis.

JUNTUNEN-YOUNGE

In terms of r_T, Juntunen and Younge appear to be similar (r_T = .246), but Figure 28 indicates just where this similarity is, and of equal importance, shows some marked differences as well. With the exception of the facial variables (Fig. 5) the discriminant analyses show these two series to be very similar. In terms of vault variables, Figure 28 also indicates a close relationship between the series, as only one of the vault variables (BAW) shows the two series to be dissimilar.

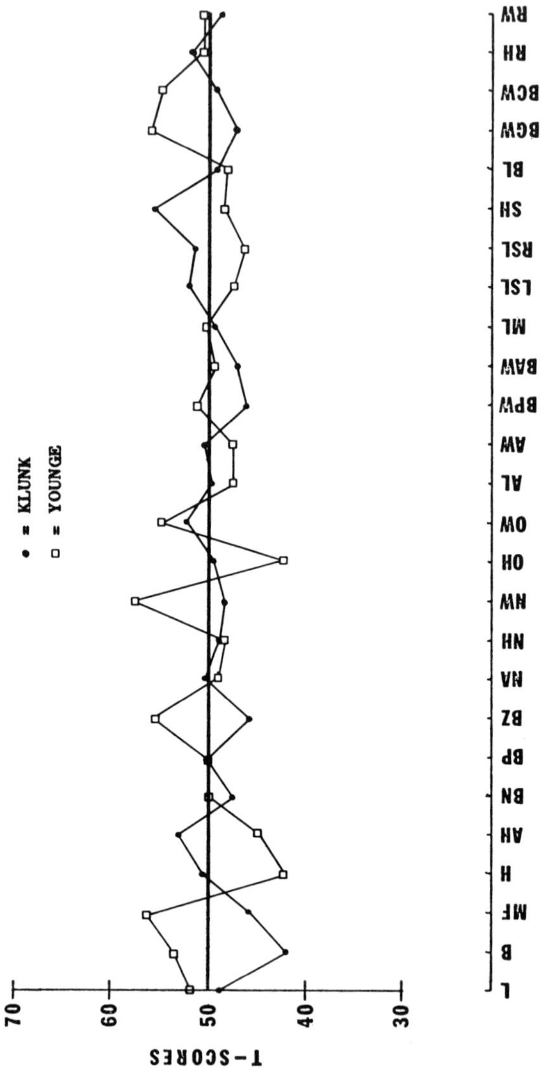

FIG. 27. Klunk-Younge Profile Pattern (r_T = -.444).

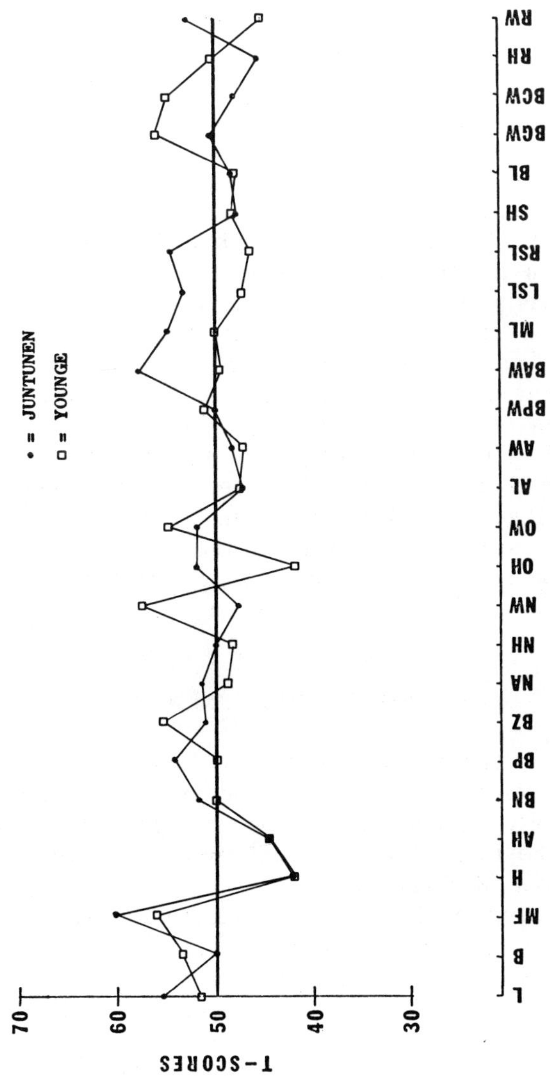

FIG. 28. Juntunen-Younge Profile Pattern (r_T = .246).

In the facial region, however, 3 of the 7 variables—NA, NW and OH—are dissimilar in their deviation from the mean. Three of the 6 mandibular variables also indicate substantial differences, the remaining 3 adding to the positive r_T value.

JUNTUNEN-SERPENT MOUNDS

Figures 9 and 11 of the discriminant analysis series suggest a certain similarity between the Juntunen and Serpent Mounds series, so the series were subjected to the profile analysis to determine the location of this similarity, and to evaluate it in terms of shape as well as size. Figure 29 illustrates the relationship between the two series, based on 15 variables.

The similarity in the shape of the vaults is immediately obvious, as none of the vault variables deviate in opposite directions from the mean. The series are also similar in the nasal region as indicated by the positions of the T-scores for the series in terms of upper facial height (NA), nasal height and nasal width. In the orbital and palate regions however, all variables show a rather marked difference. There would thus appear to be a close overall relationship between the Juntunen and Serpent Mounds series. Considering the Juntunen-Younge similarities discussed above, it is not surprising that Serpent Mounds also has some similarity with the Younge series (r_T = .239).

BUSSINGER-JUNTUNEN

Figure 30 illustrates the profile patterns of the Juntunen and Bussinger series, these patterns having a correlation coefficient of -.084. There are obvious differences and similarities in all of the cranial regions between these two Late Woodland groups from Michigan.

Of the 11 vault variables, 5 contribute negatively, 3 positively and the remaining 3 have no contribution. It is only in cranial height (H, AH) and biasterionic width that the series are similar in the vault region. Moving down to the facial region, 3 of the 7 variables deviate similarly (NA, AL, AW), the remaining nasal and orbital variables exhibiting considerable disagreement. The overall contribution of the mandibular variables is negative, as is the case in most of the other mandibular comparisons.

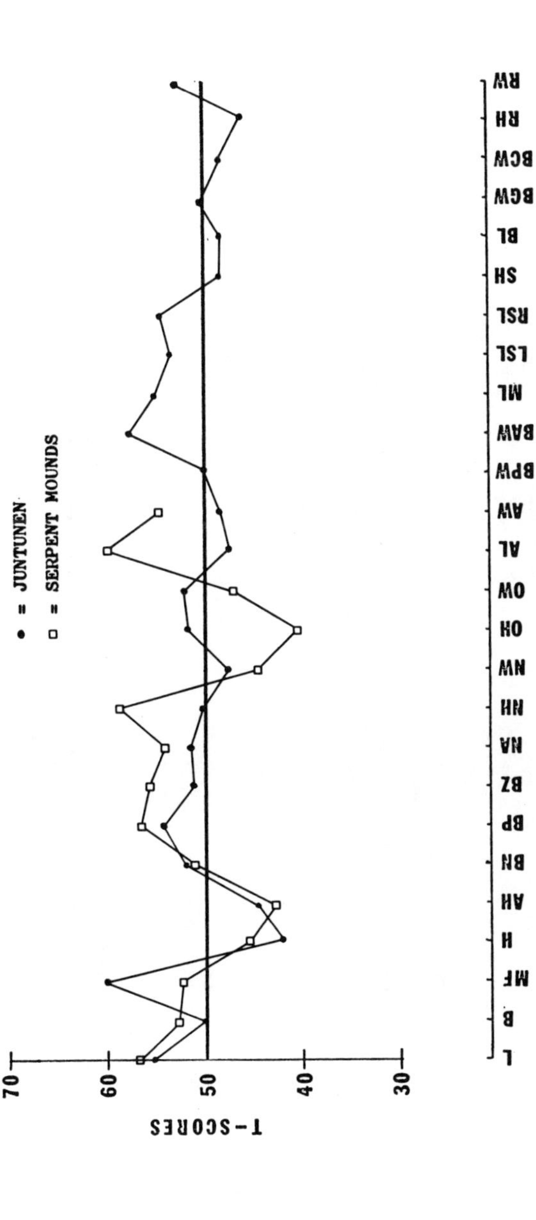

FIG. 29. Juntunen-Serpent Mounds Profile Pattern (r_T = .342).

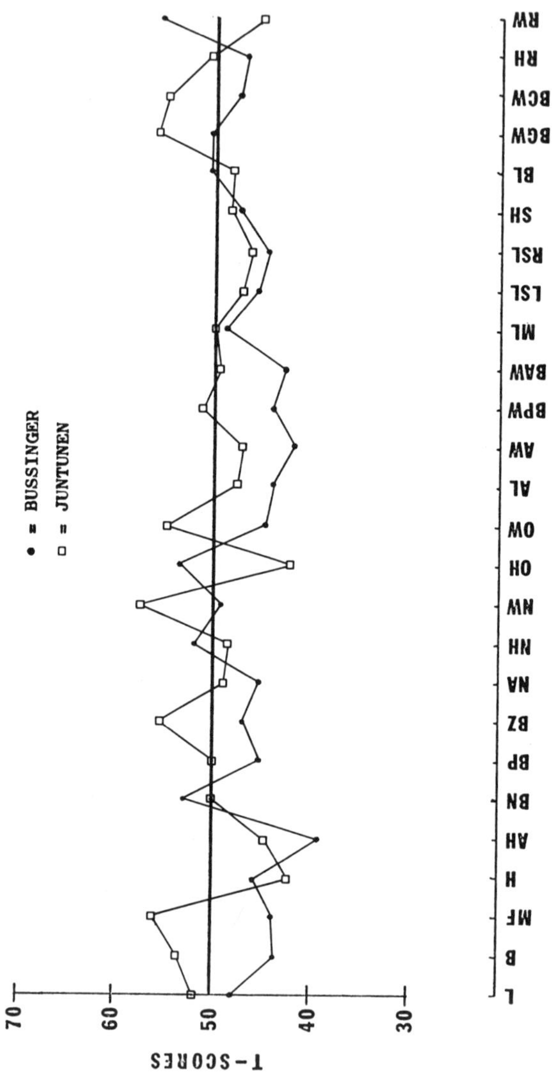

FIG. 30. Bussinger-Juntunen Profile Pattern (r_T = -.084).

BUSSINGER-FORT WAYNE

The results of the discriminant analyses are inconclusive as regards the Bussinger-Fort Wayne relationship. While Figure 10, based on facial variables, shows the two to be quite close, this similarity is not maintained in Figure 11, which is based on a combination of facial and vault variables. In terms of shape comparisons, however, the two series are quite obviously similar, at least in terms of the correlation coefficient, as $r_T = .485$.

Figure 31 indicates the causes of this relatively high (but non-significant) correlation. Unlike the other profile patterns examined here, in which a positive value of r_T was due to similar deviations both above and below the mean T-score, the correlation in the Bussinger-Fort Wayne comparison is clearly due to the fact that both series fall consistently below the mean. Only in the case of one variable, nasal height, do both series have T-scores above 50.0.

Among the 8 vault variables, only basion-nasion length contributes negatively to the correlation coefficient. While the other vault variables show marked differences in overall patterning, they are all below the mean in both series, and thus similar. In the facial region there are two dissimilarities, involving upper facial height and orbital height.

It is evident from the two types of analyses that the differences between Bussinger and Fort Wayne are primarily size differences, the series being quite similar in terms of shape. For the most part there is considerable agreement between the T-score and discriminant analyses, but the Bussinger-Fort Wayne case is an exception. Archaeologically the two sites are quite definitely related, but an earlier Middle Woodland component at the Bussinger site points to a relationship with Illinois Hopewellian groups as well.

ILINID-LENID

The final illustration of the profile patterns involves the comparison of Neumann's Ilinid and Lenid varieties (Fig. 32). The correlation coefficient of the patterns is positive, high, and significant ($r_T = .571$), even though based on only 18 variables. Looking first at the 7 vault variables, there are 3 which add to this positive correlation, maximum breadth, minimum frontal and bizygomatic breadth. There are only 2 variables which contribute

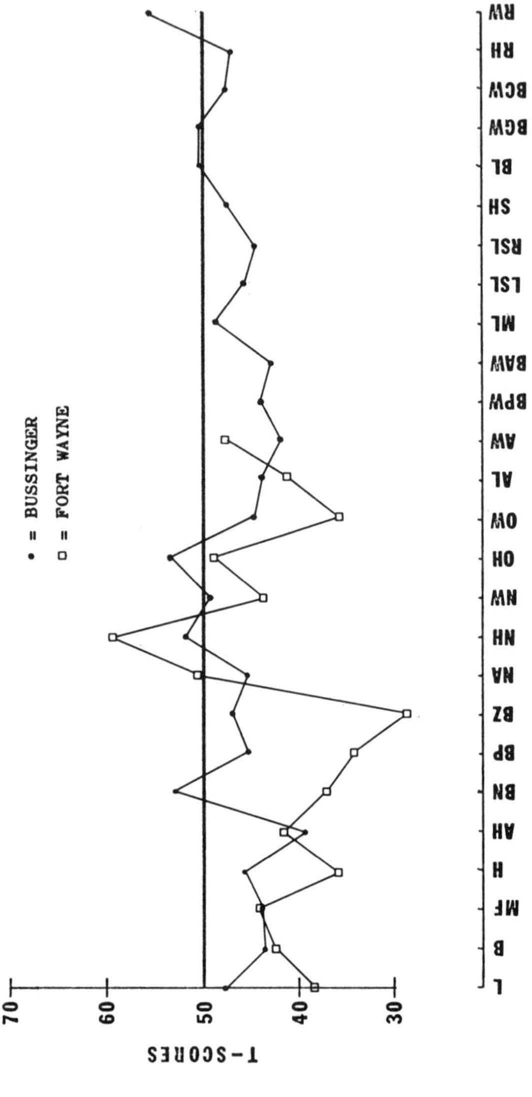

FIG. 31. Bussinger-Fort Wayne Profile Pattern (r_T = .485).

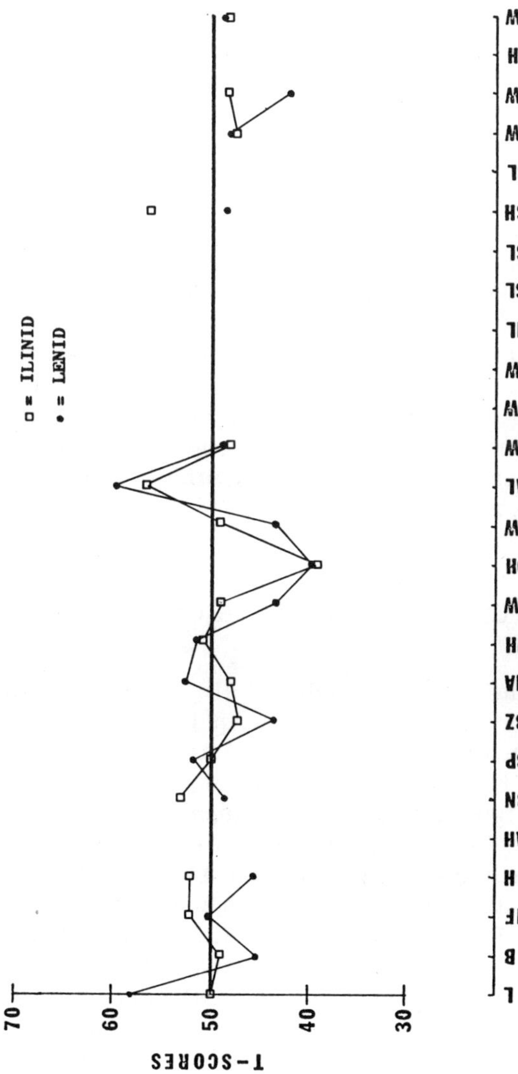

FIG. 32. Ilinid-Lenid Profile Pattern (r_T = .571).

negatively in the series, basion-bregma height and basion-nasion length. The remaining 2 variables have a zero contribution.

While the vaults of the two series are slightly more similar than different in terms of the number of variables involved, it is clear from Figure 32 that the faces are very similar, approaching identity in several variables. Of the 7 facial variables, only in upper facial height do the 2 series deviate in opposite directions from the mean. In the mandibular region the series differ in symphasis height, but the other 3 variables result in positive contributions to r_T.

The pattern analysis thus emphasizes the Ilinid-Lenid similarity which the discriminant analysis suggested (Figs. 10 and 11). Considering this similarity in size and especially in shape, the designation of the two series as physical varieties is very questionable. While Neumann sees the Lenid-Ilinid relationship as one in which the latter developed from the former, they are still considered distinct enough to warrant the varietal designation (Neumann, 1960). Considering that these two varieties are in fact more similar to each other than are most of the other series, most if not all of which are supposedly Ilinid, the establishment of these two varieties is simply not reasonable in terms of the metric data.

ANALYSIS OF NON-METRIC VARIABLES

Fourteen non-metric variables, all of which could be categorized as either present or absent in their expression, were used in the comparison of seven skeletal series. The series include Norton, Knight, Klunk, Juntunen, Younge, Bussinger and Steuben. The significance of the comparisons was tested by the Chi-square test. Two-by-two tables were constructed, comparing each site with the others, for all 14 variables. For the tables in which all cells had more than 5 entries, a computer program (CHITAB), provided by the University of Michigan Statistical Laboratory, was used. For those tables in which any one cell had 1 to 5 observations, Yates' correction (Garrett, 1958:258) was used to correct for the discontinuity of the normal curve brought about by the use of small sample sizes. Chi-square values were not calculated for those tables containing empty, or zero, cells.

The comparisons based on three of the variables, pterion form, epipteric bones and superior sagittal sinus direction, show no significant differences between any of the seven series. Two significant differences were encountered in the presence of a nasal gutter, occurring in the Norton-Knight and Norton-Younge comparisons. There were also two significant differences involving the presence of the parietal notch bone, these occurring between Juntunen and Klunk and Bussinger and Klunk.

Occipital suture wormian bones and ante-mortem tooth loss each accounted for 3 significant differences. For wormian bones, the Bussinger-Norton, -Knight and -Steuben comparisons exhibited significant differences, while the Younge-Knight, -Norton and -Bussinger comparisons were significantly different in terms of tooth loss. The presence of the mandibular torus accounts for 4 significant differences, all involving the Knight series.

Three of the variables each account for 5 significant differences. The presence of auditory exostoses reveals significant differences between Knight and Klunk and between Norton and Younge, as well as in the Younge-Klunk, -Bussinger and -Steuben comparisons. The 5 differences in concavo-convex nasal form are: Bussinger-Klunk, Bussinger-Knight, Steuben-Klunk, Steuben-Knight and Steuben-Juntunen.

The presence of dental caries brought about significant differences in 8 comparisons: Klunk is significantly different from all but Bussinger and Bussinger is different from Norton, Juntunen and Younge. Finally, 10 differences are due to the presence of the palatine torus.

Table 13 provides a summary of the non-metric variable analysis. The upper right half of the table indicates which of the variables bring about a significant difference between the two sites in question, and the lower left half indicates the number of significantly different variables for each comparison.

Of a total of 253 Chi-square comparisons, only 51 were significant at or beyond the .05 level. This might indicate a general similarity between the various series for these 14 variables, but Table 13 shows that 34 of the 51 significant differences involve either the Knight or the Klunk series. These are the largest series in terms of sample sizes, so it would seem that there is little reason to have a great deal of confidence in the results of this analysis.

If the results show any particular pattern, it is largely opposite to the implications of the metric analyses. In terms of the number of significant differences, Knight and Klunk, which were shown to be very close in the previous analyses, are quite distinct in terms of non-metric variables, and exactly the opposite is the case involving Knight and Juntunen.

TABLE 13

NON-METRIC VARIABLE COMPARISONS

	Knight	Klunk	Norton	Juntunen	Younge	Bussinger	Steuben
Knight	---	3,7,8, 9,11	4,13	8	4,7,9, 12	4,5,6, 7,8	5,8
Klunk	(5)	---	4,9,11	10,11	3,4,11	3,4,5, 10	3,5,7, 11
Norton	(2)	(3)	---	0	3,9,12, 13	6,11	0
Juntunen	(1)	(2)	(0)	---	4	4,11	5
Younge	(4)	(3)	(4)	(1)	---	9,11,12	4,7
Bussinger	(5)	(4)	(2)	(2)	(3)	---	4,6
Steuben	(2)	(4)	(0)	(1)	(2)	(2)	---

Key: 1 = pterion form; 2 = epipteric bones; 3 = auditory exostoses; 4 = palatine torus; 5 = nasal form; 6 = wormian bones; 7 = asterionic bones; 8 = mandibular torus; 9 = tympanic dehiscence; 10 = parietal notch bone; 11 = dental caries; 12 = ante-mortem tooth loss; 13 = nasal gutter; 14 = sagittal sinus direction. The upper right half of the table indicates the variables which are significantly different between sites. The lower left half indicates the number of significant differences between the sites.

Two of the variables, dental caries and ante-mortem tooth loss, were included in hopes of finding adaptational differences in terms of dental pathology. As Table 14 shows, however, there is no apparent direction in the frequencies of either variable. There is no evidence, for example, that the earlier populations had less (or more) pathology than the later ones, nor that Michigan populations were different from those of Illinois.

TABLE 14

DENTAL PATHOLOGY FREQUENCIES*
(In Percents)

	Knight	Klunk	Norton	Juntunen	Younge	Bussinger	Steuben
Carries	32.4	75.0	11.8	11.8	29.6	57.1	29.4
Loss	40.5	50.0	38.5	52.6	77.8	40.0	41.2

*Frequency is based on the number of individuals, not the number of teeth.

It would thus seem that the use of these non-metric variables is not warranted with the restricted sample sizes available in this study. While the discriminant and T-score analyses are useful in dealing with all but the smallest sample sizes, the same is not true of the non-metric analysis, and the conclusions must therefore be based primarily upon the results of the metric analysis.

III

SUMMARY AND CONCLUSIONS

THE first of several problems with which this study deals involves the biological position of the Norton Mounds skeletal series relative to Illinois and Michigan Middle and Late Woodland populations. The results of both the size and shape analyses tend to emphasize the unrelatedness of the Norton series, at least as far as the other series are concerned. Considering all of the discriminant analyses, an overall impression of isolation is most readily apparent, although a certain similarity (or lack of dissimilarity) to the Illinois groups is also apparent, especially to the Knight series. This similarity is evident in the discriminant analyses involving a combination of vault and facial variables, and especially when vault variables alone are employed. This similarity in vault variables is further refined in the profile pattern analysis, and it is obvious that the similarity is based primarily on measurements of cranial height, length and frontal diameter. In terms of facial variables, the Norton series is clearly oriented toward the Bussinger and Fort Wayne series, both of which are Michigan Late Woodland groups.

The vault variables which indicate a relationship between Norton and the Illinois series are those which are most affected by deformation, although the same basic vault shape is apparently characteristic of undeformed Hopewellian crania as well, but to a lesser degree. This being the case, an admittedly unknown portion of the Norton-Illinois similarity is due to cultural factors. This culturally-imposed similarity masks whatever genetic similarity there may be between these series, although the evidence from the cranial regions not affected by deformation points to the fact that Norton is dissimilar to the Illinois series.

Concerning the question of direct migration of the Norton group from Illinois, the results presented here can only be described as inconclusive. It must be remembered that none of the Illinois series could be the actual population from which the Norton group may have been derived, due to the fact that Norton is as early or earlier in time than any of the Illinois groups here studied. If it is assumed that Klunk and Knight are fairly representative of Middle to early Late Woodland populations from the Calhoun County area of Illinois, the fact that the Norton series is not particularly similar to these groups does not disprove migration, *per se*. At this point, it can only be implied that the Norton group did not enter Michigan from *southern* Illinois. What is needed to make a more definitive statement concerning the migration of the Norton group are Hopewellian and Early Woodland skeletal series from northeastern Illinois and northern Indiana, as well as *any* Early to Late Woodland populations from southwestern Michigan. It should be recalled that the archaeological evidence points to a close cultural relationship between Norton and *northern* Illinois Hopewellian groups. If the Norton population did migrate from northern Illinois, either the Hopewellian populations of northern and southern Illinois are very different biologically, or the Norton population is unrepresentative of Illinois Hopewellian populations in general.

While the evidence thus tends to argue against a direct migration, at least from southern Illinois, it is also clear that the Norton series is not totally unrelated to the various Illinois series. The evidence also implies that the Norton series is not like typical Michigan Late Woodland populations. There would, in fact, seem to be no typical Michigan Late Woodland populations. The similarities evident between Norton and Bussinger in terms of facial variables would seem to be very significant, considering that the Norton and Bussinger sites are the only Michigan sites employed in this study which have definite cultural connections with Illinois Hopewell. This Norton-Bussinger relationship takes on added significance considering the similarity between Bussinger and the Knight, Klunk and Frederick series, indicated in Figures 4, 9 and 11 of the discriminant analyses. As was mentioned above, the Norton series also exhibits some similarities to the Fort Wayne series. The Fort Wayne cultural material suggests influences from outside of the Michigan area (Halsey, 1968:143), as is true of the Bussinger site. It would seem significant that the two Michigan Late Woodland sites which show some biological relatedness to the Norton group are characterized by cultural influences from the south.

The Michigan Late Woodland series, Juntunen and Younge, were shown to be similar by both the discriminant and profile pattern analyses. The similarity between these two series is basically in the vault region; neither series is deformed. It is at first difficult to explain this similarity, considering the geographical distinctness of the two series (see map, Fig. 1). The inclusion of a third series, however, makes the similarity of the Juntunen-Younge relationship more understandable. This third series is from the Serpent Mound site in eastern Ontario. The series is representative of the Middle Woodland (Point Peninsula) occupation of the Serpent Mound site, and exhibits metric similarity to both Juntunen and Younge in terms of the T-score analysis, and to Juntunen in the discriminant analysis. The observed similarity between Juntunen and Serpent Mounds has archaeological documentation as well:

> The orientation of the Juntunen site was rather unspecific in the Mackinac phase, inclined more to Wisconsin in the Bois Blanc phase, but shifted strongly in the opposite direction, toward the area of incipient Iroquois-style pottery development, in the Juntunen phase (McPherron, 1967:279).

There is considerable temporal difference between the Serpent Mounds series and the Michigan Late Woodland series, so the similarity would not imply direct gene flow. The similarity is instead more likely due to slow westward movement of proto-Iroquoian groups. The orientation of the Juntunen site during the Bois Blanc phase toward Wisconsin may explain the Juntunen-Backlund similarities evident in the profile pattern analysis.

Figure 33 summarizes the relationships suggested by the results of the various analyses. It must be emphasized that the dashed lines represent only metric similarity, although gene flow might be implied in several cases. In no instance, however, can direct migration be implied; the line connecting Norton and the five Illinois sites indicates only that some similarity is evident between most of these sites, the temporal relationships being such that migration from southern Illinois is impossible.

The overall impression regarding the several relationships expressed in Figure 33 is that of two primary sources of influence affecting the Michigan series. The first of these influences is seen as coming from the Illinois area, and is evident in the Norton and Bussinger series. The second major source of genetic influence is seen as coming into the Michigan area from the northeast, here represented by the Serpent Mounds series. This northeastern influence is evident in two widely separated and ecologically distinct areas, the Straits of Mackinac (Juntunen) and southeastern Michigan (Younge). There should be intermediate groups between the Michigan and Ontario series, and the various Ontario ossuaries would be the logical choice for these intermediate populations.

The results of the discriminant and profile pattern analyses are in general agreement, and these results point to the existence of basically two rather inclusive physical types, quite distinct geographically and ecologically, but exhibiting wide temporal

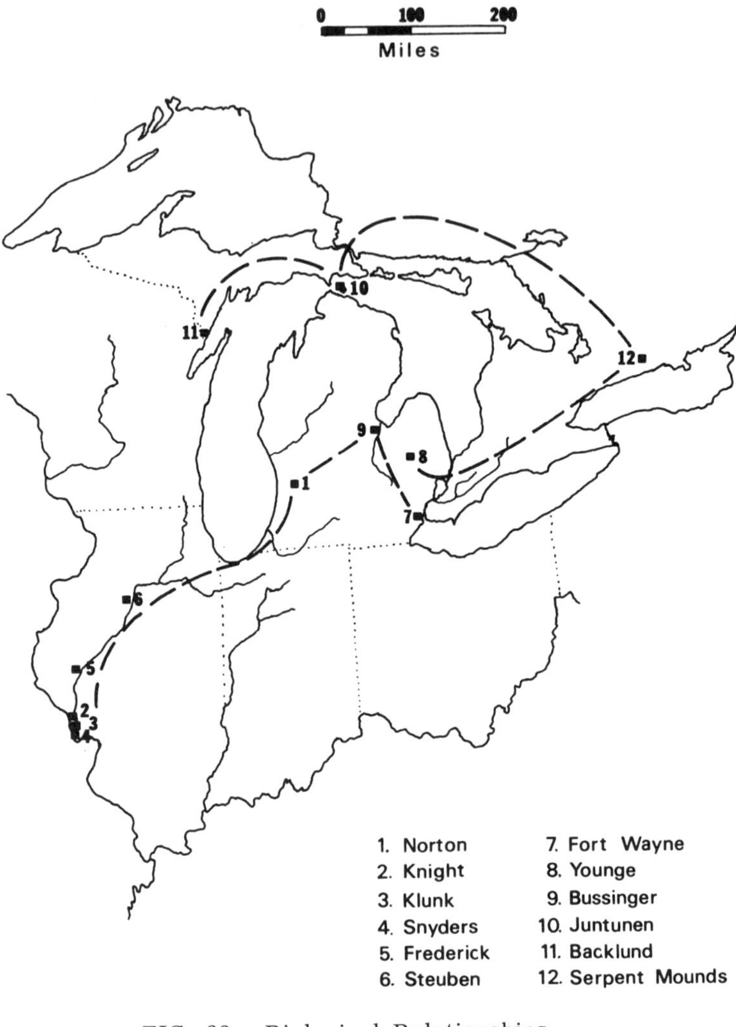

FIG. 33. Biological Relationships.

variation. The first of these includes the Knight, Klunk, Frederick, Norton, Bussinger and perhaps the Fort Wayne Mound series. The Ohio Hopewell series from the Turner site also shows some similarity to this constellation, especially in terms of the T-score analysis. This may indicate a basic similarity between Ohio and Illinois Hopewellian populations, but such a conclusion is extremely tenuous, based as it is on such a small and possibly unrepresentative Ohio Hopewellian series. The second group would include the Serpent Mounds, Juntunen and Younge series. The Backlund series is in general more similar to this second group than to the first, and a comparison of the two types of analyses indicates that the dissimilarity between Backlund and this second group is due to factors of size, not shape.

The Snyders and Steuben series are not assignable to either group on the basis of the data available. The Steuben material is simply too incomplete for the analysis, but should undoubtedly be placed within the group containing the other Illinois series. In the discriminant analysis, Figure 8 points to a close relationship between Steuben and Norton on the basis of the post-cranial remains, but it should be recalled that this analysis could show no significant differences between any of the groups tested. Archaeologically, the Snyders series should also be included in this same group, but both analyses indicate that its similarity is clearly with the Juntunen-Younge-Serpent Mounds group. Snyders thus remains problematical, suffering from both heterogeneity and small sample size.

While the statistical existence of these two large populations or series constellations may be suggested by the results of the analyses, it is of equal importance to emphasize their inclusiveness and the large amount of overlap between them. They have not been given a name in this study, because to do so serves only to emphasize their exclusiveness and prevent an understanding of possible adaptations.

Both the discriminant analysis and the profile pattern analysis indicate that Neumann's Lenid and Ilinid varieties are too similar to each other to warrant varietal classification. While it should be pointed out that these varieties are defined on a non-metric basis, many of the traits used to define them are in fact quantitative, with observations being expressed as small, medium, or large instead of using absolute measurements.

The geographical positions of the sites within the two large groups correspond quite well to major ecological differences within the Great Lakes region. The northern group, consisting of Juntunen, Serpent Mounds, Younge and Backlund are, with the exception of the Younge series, within the Lake Forest zone. The forest zone of the Canadian biotic province is dependent upon the effects of the Great Lakes for its formation, hence the term Lake Forest (Potzger, 1946). A basic cultural similarity among Indian groups inhabiting the Lake Forest has been recognized by Ritchie (1965:83), and the results of this study indicate a biological similarity between these groups as well. That the

Younge series shows biological similarities to the Lake Forest groups, yet is geographically south of the Lake Forest zone would suggest their relatively recent arrival in southeastern Michigan from the northeast.

It was emphasized above that the two major groups exhibit a considerable amount of overlap. The inclusiveness of these groups is understandable when the early movement of groups with Illinois Hopewellian influences into Michigan is considered. There is also linguistic evidence which equates Proto-Algonquian with faunal and floral assemblages which are characteristic of the Lake Forest formation (Siebert, 1967). This evidence would thus point to a western Ontario "homeland" of Algonquian-speaking groups. The assumed movement of some of these groups southward, while others remained within the Lake Forest zone, could explain some of the differences and similarities seen in the two series constellations indicated in this study.

By considering the various relationships in terms of distinct cranial regions it becomes clear that relationships established on the basis of one cranial region may not correspond to those derived from another region. It was shown in the discriminant analyses (Figures 3 through 8) that the ability to discriminate between populations decreases as one moves from the vault to the face, mandible and finally the post-cranial skeleton. This decreasing discriminatory ability, as evidenced by the fewer number of significant differences between skeletal series, is matched quite closely with increasing variability of the measurements. As measured by the coefficient of variation, variability increases steadily from the vault to the face and the mandible (Fig. 2). The causes of this increased variability are unclear, but a relationship between variability and adaptational response, on the one hand, and differing growth rates, on the other, was noted. It was thus shown that the cranial regions with the higher variability are precisely those which are characterized by a more intense adolescent growth spurt. The assumption that higher variability might also be associated with adaptational response would also seem to be reasonable, if not clearly demonstrated. We could thus expect measurements involving skeletal areas functionally and structurally related to the dentition to exhibit more variability than the major dimensions of the cranial vault, to the extent that the facial and mandibular areas are under more muscular stress and respond more readily to individual behavioral differences than is true for the vault.

The results of this study further indicate that small samples can be dealt with quite adequately. The question of the accuracy and feasibility of the analysis must be answered in terms of the relationships previously established archaeologically. Thus if the results of the skeletal analyses point out at least some of the relationships which are evident culturally, we can assume that the methods are adequate for handling the data. Happily, such is the case with many, but not all, of the relationships indicated in this study.

As is the case in many studies of this type, some questions are left unanswered and some new ones appear. The position of the Ohio Hopewellian series needs clarification, and the inclusion of the Ontario ossuaries might clarify the relationships in the southeastern Michigan area. It would also be interesting to compare some of the Wisconsin series with those used in this study.

What is needed, in short, are more carefully documented skeletal series from all over the Great Lakes area, and perhaps more interaction between those who have access to the skeletal material that does exist. Physical anthropology now has the tools to handle systematically and successfully the skeletal data that has accumulated for so many years, much of which now lies hidden on museum shelves.

APPENDIX

Many of the advanced statistical procedures now available for the analysis of skeletal material require individual measurements as input data. Such data are, however, practically nonexistent in the literature. In an admittedly modest attempt to rectify this situation, and in hopes that others will do the same, measurements of all adult males and females are listed in the following tables, as are means and standard deviations for each series. Measurements followed by an asterisk are those which were predicted by the regression analysis program described in Chapter I.

TABLE A1

NORTON CRANIAL MEASUREMENTS

Cat. No.	L	B	MF	H	AH	B-N	B-P	BZ	NA
MALES									
C16	176*	143	101	143	124*	104	97	143	82
C17	184	130	92	-	-	105*	108*	137	68
H1	187*	145	93	151	128*	103	105	135	71
H2	198	147	98	164	132	103*	110*	139	74
M1	165	141	91	138	128	92	95	140	71
M2	180	145	92	144	131	109	103	145	68
M3	172	143	94	135	120*	107	109	140	63
M6	179	141	89	146	128	110	106	139	75
N	8	8	8	7	7	8	8	8	8
Mean	180.1	141.9	93.8	145.9	127.3	104.1	104.1	139.7	71.5
S.D.	9.96	5.22	3.92	9.55	4.11	5.57	5.52	3.15	5.68
FEMALES									
I9	-	-	-	-	-	-	-	-	-

Cat. No.	NH	NW	OH	OW	AL	AW	BPW	BAW	ML
MALES									
C16	57	22	37	45	51	73	127	108	174*
C17	55*	28	41	46	62	64	118*	107*	181*
H1	54	25	34	42	53	63	130	115*	184*
H2	55	26	36	41	58	70*	130*	118*	194*
M1	51	27	38	37	57	65	127	111	162
M2	53	25	38	42	50	62	128	119	179
M3	50	30	35	37	54	68	127*	113*	170*
M6	53	24	34	38	53	68	128	111	176
N	8	8	8	8	8	8	8	8	8
Mean	53.5	25.9	36.6	41.0	54.8	66.6	126.9	112.7	177.5
S.D	2.27	2.48	2.39	3.46	3.99	3.78	3.80	4.37	9.56
FEMALES									
19	-	-	-	-	-	-	-	-	-

Cat.. No.	LSL	RSL	SH	BL	BGW	BCW	RH	RW
MALES								
C16	87	97	37	96	104	125	73	35
C17	-	-	36	99	108	131	63	36
H1	88*	90	34	89	101	124	67	36
H2	90*	92	35	100	109	140	60	37
M1	79	81	39	90	96	122	75	33
M2	91	100	37	98	103	132	73	37
M3	86*	87	30	99	102*	122*	-	37
M6	79	78	38	93	102	124	60	34

TABLE A1: (Continued)

Cat. No.	LSL	RSL	SH	BL	BGW	BCW	RH	RW
C15	-	-	32	91	-	-	55	36
J6	-	-	30	99	108*	131	64	36
N	7	7	10	10	9	9	9	10
Mean	85.7	89.3	34.8	95.4	103.7	127.9	65.6	35.7
S.D.	4.89	7.99	3.23	4.25	4.15	6.03	6.93	1.34
FEMALES								
19	-	-	31	89	95	130	56	36

TABLE A2

NORTON POST-CRANIAL MEASUREMENTS

Cat. No.	HL	HHD	HA-P	HM-L	RL	UL	CL	FL	FBL
MALES									
C15	312	43	20	22	246	265	149	447	441
C17	357	48	20	25	260	277	165	-	-
M1	340	48	21	22	256	276	161*	477	473
M2	346	50	21	22	274*	291	158	453	450
M6	355	42	20	20	-	-	163*	473	469
N	5	5	5	5	4	4	5	4	4
Mean	342.0	46.2	20.4	22.2	259.0	277.5	159.2	462.5	458.3
S.D.	18.55	3.86	0.58	1.00	14.19	13.05	2.75	14.73	15.26
FEMALES									
19	314	38	19	22	238	256	-	451	452

Cat. No.	FHD	FA'-P'	FM'-L'	FA-P	FM-L	TL	TL'	TA-P	TM-L
MALES									
C15	45	30	34	30	26	381	375*	38	26
C17	53	32	36	32*	31*	-	-	43	30
M1	50	28	31	30	27	390	386*	37	25
M2	50	30	28	32	29	394	388*	39	27
M6	48	26	29	28	25	397	393*	34	28
N	5	5	5	5	5	4	4	5	5
Mean	49.5	29.5	31.6	30.4	27.6	390.5	385.5	38.2	27.2
S.D.	2.36	1.92	2.65	1.63	1.71	6.95	7.59	2.16	1.29
FEMALES									
19	43	27	32	29	27	377	372	37	26

TABLE A3

NORTON MALE CRANIAL INDICES

Cat. No.	L/B	H/L	H/B	MF/B	BZ/B	L+B+H/3	OH/OW	NW/NH	NA/BZ	BP/BN	MF/BZ
H1	77.5	80.7	104.1	64.1	93.1	161.0	81.0	46.3	52.6	101.9	68.9
H2	74.2	82.8	111.6	66.7	94.6	169.7	87.8	47.3	53.2	106.8	70.5
M1	85.5	83.6	97.9	64.5	99.3	148.0	102.7	52.9	50.7	103.3	65.0
M2	80.6	80.0	99.3	63.4	100.0	156.3	90.5	47.2	46.9	94.5	63.4
M3	83.1	78.5	94.4	65.7	97.9	150.0	94.6	60.0	45.0	101.9	67.1
M6	78.8	81.6	103.5	63.1	98.6	155.3	89.5	45.3	54.0	96.4	64.0
C16	81.3	81.3	100.0	70.6	100.0	154.0	82.2	38.6	57.3	93.3	70.6
C17	70.7	-	-	70.8	105.4	-	89.1	50.9	49.6	102.9	67.2
N	8	7	7	8	8	7	8	8	8	8	8
Mean	79.0	81.2	101.5	66.1	98.6	156.3	89.7	48.6	51.2	100.1	67.1
S.D.	4.80	1.71	5.53	3.06	3.73	7.26	6.86	6.25	3.98	4.79	2.80

TABLE B1

KNIGHT CRANIAL MEASUREMENTS

Cat. No.	L	B	MF	H	AH	B-N	B-P	BZ	NA
MALES									
380198	176	143	96	149	127	105	97	141	76
380197	179	135	87	141	122	106	101	133	77
380196	180	141	88	145	126	108	101	145	74
380279	176	156	95	142*	123	104*	97*	147	76
380286	178	141	98	147	123	111	100	143	77*
380088	193	137	103	146	125	116	113	147*	79
380200	179	135	94	143	128	106*	100*	140*	-
380287	176	-	90	-	-	104*	98*	-	70*
380274	172	134	99	130	113	102	96	127	70
380087	190	137	94	141	122	105	100	141	72
380098	180	131	89	146	121	108	106	135	75
380193	181	138	95	145	123	108	103	142	76
380096	182	151	98	151	137	111	101	149	69
380089	179	134	89	151	125	104	97	134	80
380083	187	141	92	143	124	103	104	140	74
380201	170	143	95	151	132	107	101	137	76
380102	188	143	86	146	124	107	98	143	72
380110	181	138	92	142	131	102	102	137	74
380296	188	133	97	137	115	101	100	139	71
380094	187	139	91	153	131	106	106	147	76
380195	175	136	98	141	118	116	98	139	71
380101	191	150	100	153	130	111	102	151	82
380085	183	133	90	144	120	102	100	140	78
380191	189	138	92	150	127	111	105	143	73
N	24	23	24	23	23	24	24	23	23
Mean	181.7	139.4	93.7	145.1	124.7	106.8	101.1	140.9	74.7
S.D.	6.22	6.21	4.4	5.43	5.52	4.14	3.79	5.60	3.39
FEMALES									
380284	169	130	87	138	115	101	95	131	76
380105	174	134	86	133	116	99	98	132	66
380103	175	143	99	142	124	99	96	135	70
380091	179	133	90	134	117	101	102	126	74
380194	174	133	89	141	123	105	101	130	70
380086	171	136	85	138	119	101	99	132	65
380084	177	135	93	136	122	100	97	130	74
380202	174	130	94	135	115	104	100	129	70
380292	180	132	95	122	114	96	93	128	66
380293	177	135	91	134	117	100	96	128	66
380298	-	132	83	141	117	98	92	125	72
380237	184	135	93	136	117	105	101	132	68
380294	165	128	84	-	104	-	-	119	62
N	12	13	13	12	13	12	12	13	13
Mean	174.9	133.5	89.9	135.8	116.9	100.8	97.5	129.0	69.2
S.D.	5.09	3.69	4.80	5.29	5.01	2.77	3.23	4.04	4.12

TABLE B1: (Continued)

Cat. No.	NH	NW	OH	OW	AL	AW	BPW	BAW	ML
MALES									
380198	55	26	38	43	51	68	127	111	172
380197	53	27	32	41	53	69	116	109	176
380196	55	26	35	43	54	66	123	110	179
380279	58	27	37	42	51	68	132	115	174
380286	58	27	38	46	52*	68*	126	109	177
380088	55	28	39	44	58	77	128	114	191
380200	-	27*	-	43*	53*	-	122	113	176
380287	54	27	35	42	53*	65*	-	104	174
380274	50	27	36	44	52*	63	110	103	171
380087	54	26	38	42	51	66*	117	115	198
380098	55	29	34	44	59	67*	117	106	178
380193	55	26	37	46	57	64	125	115	179
380096	50	28	35	44	50	68	136	122	179
380089	54	24	37	44	52	70	122	112	176
380083	52	23	34	44	53	65	120	117	185
380201	56	29	38	44	54*	70	127	118	168
380102	52	23	37	42	53	69	128	118	185
380110	54	25	37	43	54	65	121	110	180
380296	51	27	32	41	54	63	122	106	184
380094	54	27	33	45	58	70	128	117	181
380195	52	26	37	45	52	62	122	110	173
380101	59	27	40	46	53	72	133	118	185
380085	54	25	38	44	54	66	120	106	182
380191	55	27	35	47	57	66	125	112	184
N	23	24	23	24	24	23	23	24	24
Mean	54.1	26.4	36.2	43.7	53.7	67.3	123.8	112.1	179.5
S.D.	2.34	1.56	2.17	1.60	2.44	3.33	5.94	5.00	6.67
FEMALES									
380284	54	22	36	42	52	59	114	105	168
380105	50	24	32	42	50	64	116	106	174
380103	50	24	35	43	53	62	124	113	173
380091	54	29	38	40	57	63	109	106	179
380194	49	26	35	44	53	61	118	110	172
380086	50	26	34	42	52	65	123	100	168
380084	52	27	36	43	53	67	119	109	175
380202	51	26	36	40	51	63	117	105	173
380292	47	23	34	40	50	54	116	107	178
380293	49	27	38	41	48	64*	112	106	175
380298	50	22	33	39	50	60*	115	103	-
380237	52	26	36	45	52	64	116	106	181
380294	45	24	34	39	49	55	110	102	164
N	13	13	13	13	13	13	13	13	12
Mean	50.2	25.1	35.2	41.5	51.5	61.6	116.1	106.0	172.0
S.D.	2.52	2.10	1.78	1.90	2.30	3.80	4.41	3.39	6.72

TABLE B1: (Continued)

Cat. No.	LSL	RSL	SH	BL	BGW	BCW	RH	RW
MALES								
380198	80	83	39	99	106	130	64	30
380197	93	91	38	100	95	116	69	38
380196	84	81	37	95	106	132	81	35
380279	80	82	-	-	-	-	-	-
380286	80	78	-	-	-	-	-	-
380088	89	89	37	115	109*	133*	73	38
380200	82	81	-	-	-	-	-	-
380287	82	80	40	101	112	-	-	33*
380274	-	-	34	90	101	114	60	32
380087	93	95	39	100*	105*	126*	-	37
380098	79	79	38	100	102	123	71	33
380193	85	81	39	93	116	133	71	32
380096	87	90	36	98	113	135	65	35
380089	83	84	38	93	102	123	71	32
380083	90	91	34	100	100	121	73	35
380201	78	83	34	97	102*	122*	-	32
380102	81	82	34	99	114	122	72	39
380110	87	88	36	98	103	123	65	36
380296	75	78	-	-	-	-	-	-
380094	91	95	-	-	-	-	-	-
380195	77	75	-	-	-	-	-	-
380101	96	92	35	105	110	136*	76	38
380085	83	86	36	100	106	126*	70	33
380191	79	82	34	100	102*	123	68	33
N	23	23	18	18	18	17	15	18
Mean	84.1	84.6	36.6	99.1	105.8	125.8	69.9	34.5
S.D.	5.71	5.69	2.06	5.30	5.58	6.46	5.16	2.66
FEMALES								
380284	80	79	40	92	99	120	58	27
380105	77	78	33	93	97	106	57	33
380103	84	84	33	94	99	124	67	30
380091	80	83	37	97	99	111	54	33
380194	82	83	35	95	103	122	59	31
380086	76	75	30	97	94	121	63	37
380084	85	83	39	87	89	122	63	30
380202	80	78	33	94	98	116	63	34
380292	79	79	32	82	99	112	62	-
380293	82	83	34	95	95	-	57	32
380298	78	79	33	85	97	115	54	28
380195	-	-	36	97	117	125	64	37
380237	86	84	-	-	-	-	-	-
380294	81	79	-	-	-	-	-	-
N	13	13	12	12	12	11	12	11
Mean	80.8	80.5	34.6	92.3	98.8	117.6	60.1	32.0
S.D.	3.00	2.91	2.94	5.00	6.67	6.09	4.17	3.26

TABLE B2

KNIGHT POST-CRANIAL MEASUREMENTS

Cat. No.	HL	HHD	HA-P	HM-L	RL	UL	CL	FL	FBL
MALES									
380111	347	46	20	21	269	289	171*	484	480
380092	327*	43*	21*	21*	258*	276*	154*	431	428
380193	330*	46*	21*	21*	258*	276*	156*	445	441
380089	321	46	23	20	264	279	172	460	457
380096	343	51	22	23	263	281	150	469	464
380101	336*	48*	21*	21*	267	284*	168	461	456
380287	305	47*	21	23	239*	257	151*	429	427
380295	327	42	20	20	250	268*	148	438	434
380108	328*	47*	21*	21*	258*	276*	162*	442	438
380296	339	48	21	22	255	276	152	458	456
380297	342	45	20	18	268	283	162	468	466
380099	339	46	22	19	257	273	153	456	453
380102	324	46	19	21	252	269	145	436	433
380191	349	48	22	23	273	286	168	487	482
380110	290	40	21	21	229	249	152	384	383
380098	336	48	22	21	272	295	161	453	450
N	16	16	16	16	16	16	16	16	16
Mean	330.2	46.1	21.1	21.0	258.3	276.1	157.8	450.1	446.8
S.D.	15.41	2.65	1.00	1.37	11.82	11.52	8.58	24.67	23.96
FEMALES									
380293	300	38	19	19	225	-	138	404	400
380298	308	41	22	19	235	249	145	434	431
380284	316	40	20	18	-	-	145	415	414
380105	286	37	20	16	227	249	139	398	393
380103	316	40	19	19	243	263	150	439	436
380091	319	40	20	20	251	270	146	438	435
380194	294	39	20	19	227	244	151	400	396
380195	316	40	19	19	223	251	152	451	441
380107	-	-	-	-	-	-	-	419	414
N	8	8	8	8	7	6	8	9	9
Mean	306.9	39.4	19.9	18.6	233.0	254.3	145.8	422.0	417.8
S.D.	12.23	1.30	0.99	1.19	10.52	9.95	5.23	19.27	18.63

TABLE B2: (Continued)

Cat. No.	FHD	FA'-P'	FM'-L'	FA-P	FM-L	TL	TL'	TA-P	TM-L
MALES									
380111	47	29	30	30	28	422	414	40	23
380092	44	29	31	29	28	372	367	36	24
380193	46	32	33	30	29	380	373	39	26
380089	45	29	31	31	27	378*	373*	36*	23*
380096	49	32	27	33	25	379*	374*	35	23
380101	48	34	32	33	27	410	404	40	30
380287	47	32	30	30	26	363	356	35	24
380295	46	29	31	29	27	380	375	36	23
380108	47	33	29	31	26	394	386	38	26
380296	47	32	30	27	28	380	374	37	26
380297	46	30	27	28	24	385	379	34	23
380099	47	31	32	30	30	369	365	35	20
380102	47	31	30	29	26	367	363	36	22
380191	47	34	31	29	30	409	404	37	25
380110	41	28	31	28	25	351	347	33	23
380098	49	35	28	32	28	384	376	37	25
N	16	16	16	16	16	16	16	16	16
Mean	46.4	31.3	30.2	29.9	27.1	382.7	376.9	36.5	24.1
S.D.	1.93	2.11	1.72	1.73	1.75	18.47	17.79	2.00	2.25
FEMALES									
380293	41	29	28	26	23	333	328	31	20
380298	42	31	30	26	25	364	359	31	22
380284	43	29	28	29	26	360	354	33	22
380105	39	26	28	24	23	337	331	-	-
380103	42	29	28	26	23	364	360	31	20
380091	43	27	28	27	25	369	364	36	22
380194	40	27	26	25	24	353	349	32	21
380195	43	31	29	28	26	367	362	32	24
380107	39	25	28	25	24	357	354	32	20
N	9	9	9	9	9	9	9	8	8
Mean	41.3	28.2	28.1	26.2	24.3	356.0	351.2	32.3	21.4
S.D.	1.66	2.11	1.05	1.56	1.23	12.91	13.16	1.67	1.41

TABLE B3

KNIGHT MALE CRANIAL INDICES

Cat. No.	L/B	H/L	H/B	MF/B	BZ/B	L+B+H/3	OH/OW	NW/NH	NA/BZ	BP/BN	MF/BZ
380198	81.3	84.7	104.2	67.1	98.6	156.0	84.3	47.3	53.9	92.4	68.1
380197	75.4	71.6	104.4	64.4	98.5	151.7	78.0	50.9	57.9	95.3	65.4
380196	78.3	80.6	102.8	62.4	102.8	155.3	81.4	47.3	51.0	93.5	60.7
380279	88.6	80.7	91.0	60.9	94.2	158.0	88.1	46.6	51.7	93.3	64.6
380286	79.2	82.6	104.3	69.5	101.4	155.3	82.6	46.6	53.8	90.1	68.5
380088	71.0	75.6	106.6	75.2	107.3	158.7	88.6	50.9	53.7	97.4	70.1
380200	75.4	79.9	98.6	69.6	103.7	152.3	-	-	-	94.3	67.1
380287	-	-	-	-	-	-	83.3	50.0	-	94.2	-
380274	77.9	75.6	97.0	73.9	94.8	145.3	81.8	54.0	55.1	94.1	78.0
380087	72.1	74.2	102.9	68.6	102.9	156.0	90.5	48.1	51.1	95.2	66.7
380098	72.8	81.1	111.5	67.9	103.1	148.7	77.3	52.7	55.6	98.1	65.9
380193	76.2	80.1	105.1	68.8	102.9	173.0	80.4	47.3	53.5	95.4	66.9
380096	83.0	83.0	100.0	64.9	98.7	161.3	79.5	56.0	46.3	91.0	65.8
380089	74.9	84.4	112.7	66.4	100.0	154.7	84.1	44.4	59.7	93.3	66.4
380083	75.4	76.5	101.4	65.2	99.3	157.0	77.3	44.2	52.9	101.0	65.7
380201	84.1	88.8	105.6	66.4	95.8	154.7	86.4	51.8	55.5	94.4	69.3
380102	76.1	77.7	102.1	60.1	100.0	159.0	88.1	44.2	50.3	91.6	60.1
380110	76.2	78.5	102.9	66.7	99.3	153.7	86.0	46.3	54.1	100.0	67.2
380296	70.7	72.9	103.0	72.9	104.5	152.7	78.0	52.9	51.1	99.0	69.8
380094	74.3	81.8	110.1	65.5	105.8	159.7	73.3	50.0	51.7	100.0	61.9
380195	77.7	80.6	103.7	72.1	102.2	150.7	82.2	50.0	51.1	98.3	70.5
380101	78.5	80.1	102.0	66.7	100.7	164.7	87.0	45.8	54.3	91.9	66.2
380085	72.7	78.7	108.3	67.7	105.3	153.3	86.4	46.3	55.7	98.0	64.3
380191	73.0	79.4	108.7	66.7	102.9	159.0	74.5	49.1	51.0	94.6	64.3
N	23	23	23	23	23	23	23	23	22	24	23
Mean	76.7	79.5	103.9	67.4	101.1	156.1	82.6	48.8	53.2	95.3	66.7
S.D.	4.38	3.99	4.78	3.79	3.42	5.61	4.73	3.26	2.86	3.05	3.69

TABLE C1

KLUNK CRANIAL MEASUREMENTS

Cat. No.	L	B	MF	H	AH	B-N	B-P	BZ	NA
MALES									
C3057	176	128	98	138	118	107	101	137	73
C3074	178	140	91	135	123	108	100	134	76
C3030	195*	126	97	134	120	108	114	143	75
C3036	187	137	91	137	121	106	110	146*	72
C3005	185	-	93	-	-	105*	102*	-	75
C3055	191	133	90	146	124	113	104	139	71
C3121	186	138	95	-	-	104	102	141*	78
C3136	177	136	95	136	122	105	98	148	74
C3120	177	135	93	142	126	104	100	136	71
C3406	175*	136	85	134	117	95	95	146	74
C3431	176*	-	92	147	130	100	96	134	78
C3409	177*	135	90	144	131	102	97	138	76
C3644	170*	149*	86	146	129	102	90	143	70
C3660	181	131	91	142	124	107	107	140	74
C3633	175	135	93	133	120	101	101	140	72
C3605	182	137	96	141	122	104	100	139	67
C3627	182	135	93	144	123	102	102	140	69
C4038	191	140	98	150	131	103	105	145	73
C4076	183	129	92	143	124	109	101*	130	72*
C3001	-	-	93	-	-	-	-	-	75
C3021	-	-	-	-	-	-	-	-	75
N	19	17	20	17	17	19	19	18	21
Mean	181.3	135.3	92.6	140.7	123.8	104.5	101.3	139.9	73.3
S.D.	6.57	5.30	3.44	5.23	4.32	3.92	5.39	4.75	2.80
FEMALES									
C3029	-	139*	91	133	120	94	100	129	68
C3052	173	144	94	130	114	98	99	140	66
C3063	162*	134	91	135	117	97	96	126	67
C3132	170	133	92	140	124	100	90	130	66
C3425	176	134	92	140	119	104	97	126	71
C3429	178	134	91	136	119	98	93	119	69
C3606	173	133	90	143	124	102	97	130	74
C3658	-	135	85	135	121	96	96	132	70
C3664	-	134*	90	-	-	-	102*	136	69
C4020	174	134	91	141	124	101	-	128	64*
C4028	179	132	87	139	124	102	102	128	69
N	8	11	11	10	10	10	10	11	11
Mean	173.1	135.1	90.4	137.2	120.6	99.2	97.2	129.5	68.5
S.D.	5.36	3.45	2.46	4.05	3.47	3.12	3.80	5.47	2.73

TABLE C1: (Continued)

Cat. No.	NH	NW	OH	OW	AL	AW	BPW	BAW	ML
MALES									
C3057	55	28	38	44	53*	63	114	106	174
C3074	54	27	35	46	53*	65	123	109	177
C3030	52	27	35	45	58	68	115	105*	191*
C3036	52	30	35	45	60	70	126	112*	185
C3005	51	26	35	47	54*	65	-	-	183
C3055	55	26	36	44	52	66	121	105	189
C3121	57	25	36	43	53	67	128	117	185
C3136	57	26	36	43	54	64	125	111	173
C3120	56	26	36	44	53	60	121	111	177
C3406	53	25	37	43	53	66*	122*	110*	173*
C3431	53	23	39	44	51	69	-	-	174*
C3409	53	27	38	42	50	67*	123	108	175*
C3644	52	23	36	43	47	65	137	122	169*
C3660	50	27	32	44	59	64	118	102	180
C3633	55	27	34	45	55	68	118	112	174
C3605	49	25	35	42	54	68	127	111	180
C3627	50	26	36	45	51	68	121	111	180
C4038	55	32	38	45	51	67	131	115	189
C4076	53	24	37	44	53*	68	115	114	184
C3001	55	29	40	44	-	67	-	109	-
C3021	53	26	34	45	-	66	-	-	-
N	21	21	21	21	19	21	17	18	19
Mean	53.3	26.4	36.1	44.1	53.4	66.2	122.6	110.6	179.6
S.D.	2.24	2.14	1.84	1.24	3.10	2.28	6.04	4.71	6.35
FEMALES									
C3029	54	28	34	42	54	65*	115	107*	-
C3052	50	26	36	43	51	69	117	112	173
C3063	49	25	36	43	54	67	121	107	161
C3132	49	26	38	44	45	63	118	106	170
C3425	54	-	37	42	49	61	117	108	176
C3429	48	23	34	42	52	61	109	105	177
C3606	52	27	37	41	52	63	118	105	172
C3658	50	25	36	41	52	62	123	110	-
C3664	49	26	33	42	56	67	122*	106*	-
C4020	47	24	36	43	-	63	118	107	172
C4028	48	28	32	42	52	65*	113	108	177
N	11	10	11	11	10	11	11	11	8
Mean	50.0	25.8	35.4	42.3	51.7	64.2	117.4	107.4	172.3
S.D.	2.37	1.62	1.86	0.91	3.02	2.64	4.03	2.11	5.23

TABLE C1: (Continued)

Cat. No.	LSL	RSL	SH	BL	BGW	BCW	RH	RW
MALES								
C3057	78	81	-	-	-	-	-	-
C3074	90	92	-	-	-	-	-	-
C3030	-	-	37	97	118	132*	-	33
C3036	82*	82	38	94	87	140	77	39
C3005	85*	85	39	98	-	-	72	36
C3055	-	-	39	100	101	122	76	36
C3121	87	90	37	100	105	126*	64	35
C3136	82	82	39	97	106	122	62	36
C3120	87	87	37	95	111	131	71	34
C3406	80	86	-	-	-	-	-	-
C3431	-	-	41	91	95	129	59	33
C3409	84	82	39	97	105	124*	-	35
C3644	89	86	-	-	-	-	-	-
C3660	76	74	39	103	109	132	70	36
C3633	83	79	39	96	103	122	67	31
C3605	87	94	34	100	108	127	68	34
C3627	88	84	34	97	91	119	58	32
C4038	92	89	34	105	111	134	74	39
C4076	93	96	-	-	-	-	-	-
C3001	81	79	35	95	113	133	62	36
C3021	-	-	39	100	102	126*	69	39
N	17	17	16	16	15	15	14	16
Mean	84.9	85.2	37.5	96.7	104.3	127.9	67.8	35.3
S.D.	4.80	5.78	2.19	5.85	8.34	5.74	6.08	2.41
FEMALES								
C3029	-	-	36	83	-	-	58	28
C3052	81	83	32	94	104	118	53	34
C3063	86	86	35	95	98	119	60	32
C3132	79	83	33	90	100	124	57	35
C3425	87	92	-	95	94	106	58	32
C3429	80	86	38	87	95	107	70	31
C3606	81	82	35	95	99	-	-	34
C3658	87	83	36	93	93	121	61	35
C3664	98	97	34	98	99	119	60	38
C4020	76	78	34	90	96	120	67	32
C4028	80	83	38	94	-	-	-	-
C4076	-	-	-	92	-	-	69	36
N	10	10	10	12	9	8	10	11
Mean	83.5	85.3	35.1	92.2	97.6	116.8	61.3	33.4
S.D.	6.28	5.46	1.97	4.11	3.43	6.59	5.58	2.73

TABLE C2

KLUNK POST-CRANIAL MEASUREMENTS

Cat. No.	HL	HHD	HA-P	HM-L	RL	UL	CL	FL	FBL
MALES									
C3030	297	45	23	21	229	252	142	420	414
C3057	330	43	21	19	258*	276	169	-	-
C3001	317	44	23	22	234	253	148*	431	427
C3036	334	46*	23*	21*	-	-	159*	459	454
C3005	366	46	23	23	-	-	-	-	-
C3121	318	42	19	20	253	269	144	435	433
C3120	331	39	20	24	252*	270	150	437	435
C3409	314	43	19	21	235	255*	153	390	384
C3627	321	42	24	16	263	280	157	449	444
C3644	332	45	22	22	255	271	160*	461	460
C3660	348	50	22	23	280*	297	158	475	469
C3633	309	43	21	23	253*	271	145	-	-
C3605	331	45	19	18	249	267	152*	444	440
C4038	358*	50	23*	23*	285*	301	176*	-	-
C3021	323	47	22	23	-	-	154	456	453
C3055	331	46	24	22	259	275	163	449	445
N	16	16	16	16	13	13	15	12	12
Mean	328.8	44.8	21.8	21.3	254.2	272.1	155.3	442.2	438.2
S.D.	17.57	2.86	1.73	2.15	16.27	14.85	9.38	22.20	22.69
FEMALES									
C3664	316	40	19	18	250	270	149	450	444
C3658	297	41	18	18	234	254	138	420	415
C3606	280	40	21	21	217	-	137	396	392
C3063	301	37	18	17	231	253	134	422	417
C3052	317	40	19	20	257	-	-	428	421
C3029	295	38	19	19	-	-	-	425	421
N	6	6	6	6	5	3	4	6	6
Mean	301.0	39.3	19.0	18.8	237.8	259.0	139.5	423.5	418.3
S.D	13.96	1.51	1.10	1.47	15.90	9.54	6.56	17.30	16.61

TABLE C2: (Continued)

Cat. No.	FHD	FA'-P'	FM'-L'	FA-P	FM-L	TL	TL'	TA-P	TM-L
MALES									
C3030	43	29	29	27	25	349	342	33	23
C3057	45	26	29	-	26*	-	-	33	23
C3001	46	28	30	29	23	355	352	31	25
C3036	46	30	31	33	29	387	383	37	25
C3005	49	33*	32*	31	30	-	-	34	24
C3121	43	29	25	26	23	370	363	30	21
C3120	43	30	30	27	26	382	375	37	24
C3409	41	32	25	25	25	-	-	33*	26*
C3627	46	34	27	28	24	398	388	36	25
C3644	46	31	28	28	26	393	386	36	26
C3660	48	33	31	29	28	-	-	36	24
C3633	43*	30*	-	-	-	-	-	-	-
C3605	45	32	29	29	27	373	365	33	23
C4038	51	36	31	34	29	443	431	46	31
C3021	48	34	31	33	27	375	372	37	27
C3055	46	33	31	30	26	-	-	38	27
N	16	16	15	14	15	10	10	15	15
Mean	45.6	31.3	29.3	29.2	26.3	382.5	375.7	35.3	24.9
S.D.	2.55	2.60	2.19	2.72	2.12	26.27	24.40	3.79	2.34
FEMALES									
C3664	42	30	28	27	23	368	364	31	22
C3658	41	27	25	26	23	364	359	30	20
C3606	42	29	26	24	25	339	335	33	24
C3063	38	28	24	23	21	353	348	28	21
C3052	41	25	28	29	22	377	371	33	24
C3029	40	31	27	27	24	-	-	-	-
N	6	6	6	6	6	5	5	5	5
Mean	40.6	28.3	26.3	26.0	23.0	360.2	355.4	31.0	22.2
S.D.	1.51	2.16	1.63	2.19	1.41	14.65	14.15	2.12	1.80

TABLE C3

KLUNK MALE CRANIAL INDICES

Cat. No.	L/B	H/L	H/B	MF/B	BZ/B	L+B+H/3	OH/OW	NW/NH	NA/BZ	BP/BN	MF/BZ
53057	72.7	78.4	107.8	76.6	107.0	147.3	86.4	50.9	53.3	94.4	71.5
53664	87.6	85.9	98.0	57.7	96.0	155.0	83.7	44.2	49.0	82.2	60.1
53074	78.7	75.8	96.4	65.0	95.7	151.0	76.1	50.0	56.7	92.6	67.9
54076	70.5	78.1	110.9	71.3	100.8	151.7	84.1	45.3	55.4	92.7	70.8
53406	77.7	76.6	98.5	62.5	103.4	148.3	86.0	47.2	50.7	100.0	58.2
53030	64.6	68.7	106.3	77.0	113.5	151.7	77.8	51.9	52.4	90.0	67.8
53431	-	83.5	-	-	-	-	88.6	43.4	58.2	96.0	68.7
53036	73.3	73.3	100.0	66.4	106.6	153.7	77.8	57.7	49.3	103.8	62.3
53005	-	-	-	-	-	-	74.5	51.0	-	97.1	-
53409	76.3	81.4	106.7	66.7	102.2	152.0	90.5	50.9	55.1	95.1	65.2
53121	74.2	-	-	68.8	102.2	-	83.7	43.9	55.3	98.1	67.4
53136	76.8	76.8	100.0	69.9	108.8	149.7	83.7	45.6	50.0	93.3	64.2
53055	69.6	76.4	109.8	67.7	104.5	156.7	81.8	47.3	51.1	92.0	64.7
53660	72.4	78.5	108.4	69.5	106.9	151.3	72.7	54.0	52.9	100.0	65.0
53633	77.1	76.0	98.5	68.9	103.7	147.7	75.6	49.1	51.4	100.0	66.4
54038	73.3	78.5	107.1	70.0	103.6	160.3	84.4	58.2	50.3	101.9	67.6
53605	75.3	77.5	102.9	70.1	101.5	153.3	83.3	51.0	48.2	96.2	69.1
53627	74.2	79.1	106.7	68.9	103.7	153.7	80.0	52.0	49.3	100.0	66.4
53120	76.3	80.2	105.2	68.9	100.7	151.3	81.8	46.4	52.2	96.2	68.4
N	17	17	16	17	17	16	19	19	18	19	18
Mean	74.7	77.9	103.9	68.6	103.6	152.2	81.7	49.5	52.3	95.9	66.2
S.D.	4.79	3.83	4.72	4.52	4.35	3.35	4.88	4.30	2.89	4.95	3.45

TABLE D1

FREDERICK CRANIAL MEASUREMENTS

Cat. No.	L	B	MF	H	AH	B-N	B-P	BZ	NA
MALES									
11SC1	184	139	88	143	120	111	100	140	76*
11SC20	175	146	91	145	124	101	96	147	68
11SCA	173	139	97	143	126	99	90	141	67
11SC14	183	141	93	142	124	105	102	142	73
11SC22	190	145	92	150	129	108	110	151	81
N	5	5	5	5	5	5	5	5	5
Mean	181.0	142.0	92.2	144.6	124.6	104.8	99.6	144.2	73.0
S.D.	6.96	3.12	3.27	3.21	3.29	4.92	7.40	4.66	5.79
FEMALE									
11SC48	165	136	91	149	134	105	102	139	79

Cat. No.	NH	NW	OH	OW	AL	AW	BPW	BAW	NL
MALES									
11SC1	58	29	37	48	57*	67*	122	111	184
11SC20	58	29	40	44	51	71	132	111	175
11SCA	51	28	36	43	46	64	118	103	171
11SC14	52	26	35	44	54	67	125	112	180
11SC22	56	28	35	43	59	73	124	108	186
N	5	5	5	5	5	5	5	5	5
Mean	55.0	28.0	36.6	44.4	53.4	68.4	124.2	109.0	179.2
S.D.	3.32	1.23	2.07	2.07	5.13	3.58	5.12	3.67	6.22
FEMALE									
11SC48	56	27	35	44	53	68	129	109	165

Cat. No.	LSL	RSL	SH	BL	BGW	BCW	RH	RW
MALES								
11SC1	79	86	40	99	100	124*	73	36
11SC20	86	90	34	101	110	133	68	35
11SCA	79	78	32	94	98	125	67	35
11SC14	82	84	-	-	-	-	-	-
11SC22	89	89	42	104	98	133*	72	39
N	5	5	4	4	4	4	4	4
Mean	83.0	85.4	37.0	99.5	101.5	128.7	70.0	36.3
S.D.	4.42	4.78	4.76	4.20	5.75	4.92	2.94	1.89
FEMALE								
11SC48	79	79	-	-	-	-	-	-

TABLE D2

FREDERICK MALE CRANIAL INDICES

Cat. No.	L/B	H/L	H/B	MF/B	BZ/B	L+B+H/3	OH/OW	NW/NH	NA/BZ	BP/BN	MF/BZ
11SC1	75.5	77.7	102.9	63.3	100.7	155.3	77.1	50.0	54.3	90.1	62.9
11SC20	83.4	82.9	99.3	62.3	100.7	155.3	90.9	50.0	46.3	95.0	61.9
11SCA	80.3	82.7	102.9	69.8	101.4	151.7	83.7	54.9	47.5	90.9	68.8
11SC14	77.0	77.6	100.7	66.0	100.7	155.3	79.5	50.0	51.4	97.1	65.5
11SC22	76.3	78.9	103.4	63.4	104.1	161.7	81.4	50.0	53.6	101.9	60.9
N	5	5	5	5	5	5	5	5	5	5	5
Mean	78.5	80.0	101.8	65.0	101.5	155.9	82.5	51.0	50.6	95.0	64.0
S.D.	3.29	2.64	1.76	3.03	1.47	3.62	5.28	2.19	3.59	4.82	3.18

TABLE E1

SNYDERS CRANIAL MEASUREMENTS

Cat. No.	L	B	MF	H	AH	B-N	B-P	BZ	NA
MALES									
380128	177	138	87	136	119	108	99*	145*	75*
380356	183	144	100	145	128	106	100	148*	77
380134	184*	144*	95	130	116	98	103	141	69
380131	179	145	99	136	121	97	100	147*	69
N	4	4	4	4	4	4	4	4	4
Mean	180.7	142.7	95.3	136.7	121.0	102.2	100.5	145.2	72.5
S.D.	3.30	3.20	5.91	6.19	5.10	5.56	1.73	3.10	4.12
FEMALE									
380129	-	143*	92	131	118	94	98	133*	69

Cat. No.	NH	NW	OH	OW	AL	AW	BPW	BAW	ML
MALES									
380128	56	26*	37*	44*	52*	65	126	110	177
380356	57	26	35	46	57*	75	129	112	182
380134	52	28	35	44	54	65	132	119*	181*
380131	52	26	36	46	53	65	127	111	177
N	4	4	4	4	4	4	4	4	4
Mean	54.3	26.5	35.8	45.0	54.0	67.5	128.5	113.0	179.2
S.D.	2.63	1.00	0.96	1.16	2.16	5.00	2.65	4.08	2.63
FEMALE									
380129	46	27	36	43	-	64	121	113	-

Cat. No.	LSL	RSL	SH	BL	BGW	BCW	RH	RW
MALES								
380128	75	83	-	-	-	-	-	-
380356	86	84	-	-	-	-	-	-
380134	-	-	-	-	-	-	-	-
380131	92	88	-	-	-	-	-	-
N	3	3	-	-	-	-	-	-
Mean	84.3	85.0	-	-	-	-	-	-
S.D.	8.62	2.65	-	-	-	-	-	-
FEMALE								
380129	85	78	-	-	-	-	-	-

TABLE E2

SNYDERS MALE CRANIAL INDICES

Cat. No.	L/B	H/L	H/B	MF/B	BZ/B	L+B+H/3	OH/OW	NW/NH	NA/BZ	BP/BN	MF/BZ
380128	78.0	76.8	98.6	63.0	105.1	150.3	84.1	46.4	51.7	91.7	60.0
380356	78.7	79.2	100.7	69.4	102.8	157.3	76.1	45.6	52.0	94.3	67.6
380134	78.3	70.7	90.3	66.0	97.9	152.7	79.5	53.8	48.9	105.1	67.4
380131	81.0	76.0	93.8	68.3	101.4	153.3	78.3	50.0	46.9	103.1	67.3
N	4	4	4	4	4	4	4	4	4	4	4
Mean	79.0	75.7	95.9	66.7	101.8	153.4	79.5	48.9	49.8	98.6	65.6
S.D.	1.36	3.59	4.70	2.83	3.01	2.91	3.37	3.76	2.43	6.55	3.72

TABLE F1

STEUBEN CRANIAL MEASUREMENTS

Cat. No.	L	B	MF	H	AH	B-N	B-P	BZ	NA
MALES									
-	-	-	90	-	-	-	-	-	73
-	191	136	92	-	-	-	-	-	-
-	-	135	91	141	123	97	-	-	-
-	-	140	85	-	-	-	-	-	-
-	-	-	91	-	-	-	-	125	65
-	175	145	91	-	-	-	-	-	-
N	2	4	6	1	1	1	-	1	2
Mean	183.0	139.0	90.0	141.0	123.0	97.0	-	125.0	69.0
S.D.	11.31	4.55	2.53	-	-	-	-	-	5.66
FEMALES									
58224	-	134	89	134	124	98	100	122	70
58226	178	128	-	138*	121	101*	-	128*	64
58225	-	129	94	148	130	112	-	137*	-
58231	-	140	91	-	136	-	-	-	69
58232	170	133	90	137*	120	103*	103*	130*	72
58238	173	122	90	-	-	-	-	-	65
58249	186	139*	89	-	-	-	-	-	-
58252	-	134*	89	-	-	-	-	-	-
58256	171	134*	89	-	-	-	102*	-	-
N	5	9	8	4	5	4	3	4	5
Mean	175.6	132.6	90.1	139.2	126.2	103.5	101.7	129.2	68.0
S.D.	6.58	5.57	1.73	6.08	6.72	6.03	1.53	6.19	3.39

TABLE F1: (Continued)

Cat. No.	NH	NW	OH	OW	AL	AW	BPW	BAW	ML
MALES									
-	55	-	38	41	-	-	-	-	-
-	-	-	-	-	-	-	-	-	187
-	-	-	-	-	55	70	125	109	-
-	-	-	-	-	-	66	-	109	-
-	49	24	35	40	53	64	-	-	-
-	-	-	-	-	61	67	130	116	173
N	2	1	2	2	3	4	2	3	2
Mean	52.0	24.0	36.5	40.5	56.3	66.8	127.5	111.3	180.0
S.D.	4.24	-	2.12	0.71	4.16	2.50	3.54	4.04	9.90
FEMALES									
58224	54	24	36	41	55	64	123	111	-
58226	45	-	37	40	-	63*	113	109	176
58225	-	-	33	38	-	66*	127	106	-
58231	50	23	37	41	-	66	-	106*	-
58232	52	27	37	37	57	64	117	106*	168
58238	47	-	39	38	-	-	-	106*	172
58249	-	27	-	-	-	62	-	112	184*
58252	-	25	-	-	-	-	-	106	-
58256	-	26	-	-	56	63	-	106*	170*
N	5	6	6	6	3	7	4	9	5
Mean	49.6	25.3	36.5	39.2	56.0	64.0	120.0	107.6	174.0
S.D.	3.65	1.63	1.98	1.72	1.00	1.53	6.22	2.46	6.33

TABLE F1: (Continued)

Cat. No.	LSL	RSL	SH	BL	BGW	BCW	RH	RW
MALES								
-	-	-	-	-	-	-	-	-
-	-	-	-	-	-	-	-	-
-	75	74	-	-	-	-	-	-
-	89	88	-	-	-	-	-	-
-	-	-	-	-	-	-	-	-
-	84	80	-	-	-	-	-	-
58243	-	-	35	95	106*	128	61	36
58255	-	-	35	90	-	-	-	-
58259	-	-	36	91	105	125	68	34
58260	-	-	34	72	103	127	72	40
58258	-	-	43	99	-	-	-	35
58242	-	-	36	96	107*	130	71	35
58251	-	-	31	69	105	123	64	34
58244	-	-	39	89	106	126	66	33
N	3	3	8	8	6	6	6	7
Mean	82.7	80.7	36.1	87.6	105.3	126.5	67.0	35.3
S.D.	7.10	7.02	3.56	11.11	1.37	2.43	4.20	2.29
FEMALES								
58224	87	91	36	86	87	112	66	34
58226	85	79	-	-	-	-	-	-
58225	82	87	-	-	-	-	-	-
58231	-	-	34	84	84	-	60	32
58232	78	72	-	-	-	-	-	-
58238	80*	81	34	90	87	111	63	-
58249	95	99	-	-	-	-	-	-
58252	93	95	33	91	101	-	52	30
58256	80*	80	35	90	-	110	68	30
58229	-	-	-	-	-	-	64	35
N	8	8	5	5	4	3	6	5
Mean	85.0	85.5	34.4	88.2	89.8	111.0	62.2	32.2
S.D.	6.28	9.10	1.14	3.03	7.63	1.00	5.67	2.28

TABLE F2

STEUBEN POST-CRANIAL MEASUREMENTS

Cat. No.	HL	HHD	HA-P	HM-L	RL	UL	CL	FL	FBL
MALES									
58258	312	41	23	15	245	268	164	442	435
58244	311	47	21	24	254	272	149	457	453
58223	352	46	21	22	269	288	160*	457	454
58234	323*	45*	22*	21*	254*	272	161*	458	456
58233	-	44*	21*	20*	-	-	152*	441	440
58242	322	44	22	23	243	263*	163	440	438
58251	309	42	18	17	231	254	146*	440	434
N	6	7	7	7	6	6	7	7	7
Mean	321.5	44.1	21.1	20.3	249.3	269.5	156.4	447.9	444.3
S.D.	16.06	2.12	1.57	3.25	12.90	11.31	7.28	8.90	9.64
FEMALES									
58249	-	41	21	17	239	258	146	-	-
58232	308	40	21	16	233	249	137	-	-
58226	-	-	-	-	242	-	145	432	431
58225	-	-	-	-	229	244	-	418	412
58254	293	37	18	18	230	-	-	394	387
58252	323	39	18	18	250	272	-	-	-
58238	-	43	-	-	244	-	144	448	440
58231	302	44	16	13	230	-	-	-	-
58224	-	-	-	-	254	270	-	-	-
N	4	6	5	5	9	5	4	4	4
Mean	306.5	40.7	18.8	16.4	239.0	258.6	143.0	423.0	417.5
S.D.	12.61	2.58	2.17	2.07	9.21	12.40	4.08	22.89	23.44

TABLE F2: (Continued)

Cat. No.	FHD	FA'-P'	FM'-L'	FA-P	FM-L	TL	TL'	TA-P	TM-L
MALES									
58258	41	29	32	31	26	378	371	38	26
58244	49	32	26	31	26	381	374	38	24
58223	45	30	32	30	30	392	385	37	25
58234	46	27	33	30	27	293	388	39	25
58233	45	24	31	28	26	369	364	37	22
58242	46	29	31	29	27	373	368*	36	22
58251	42	26	29	23	27	351	346	30	22
N	7	7	7	7	7	7	7	7	7
Mean	44.9	28.1	30.6	28.9	27.0	376.7	370.9	36.4	23.7
S.D.	2.67	2.67	2.37	2.80	1.41	14.45	14.01	2.99	1.70
FEMALES									
58249	-	-	-	-	-	-	-	-	-
58232	-	23	30	-	-	358	354	32	22
58226	44	22	33	22	25	370	362	34	23
58225	40	21	30	24	22	342	332	30	22
58254	41	28	27	23	24	344	341	30	20
58252	-	29	26	24	24	-	-	-	-
58238	42	23	32	30	25	358	355	36	26
58231	38	19	22	-	-	350	344	22	17
58224	40	22	28	-	-	-	-	32	20
N	6	8	8	5	5	6	6	7	7
Mean	40.83	23.37	28.5	24.6	24.0	353.7	348.0	30.9	21.4
S.D.	2.04	3.42	3.55	3.13	1.23	10.46	10.97	4.45	2.82

TABLE G1

BUSSINGER CRANIAL MEASUREMENTS

Cat. No.	L	B	MF	H	AH	B-N	B-P	BZ	NA
MALES									
69857	184	133	89	131	119	104	110	137*	69
70421	185	140	94	139	114	108	101	143*	75
70430	176	129	90	139*	110	103*	98*	136*	65
70436	184	139	95	137	123	117	102*	142*	-
70483	176	139	99	138	116	104	97*	148*	70*
70482	195	137	91*	-	-	104*	104*	137	74*
70460	180	141	96	-	-	107*	100*	144*	78
70422	186	131*	91*	136	117	114	96	137*	76
69861	183	-	91	130	117*	103*	97*	-	70
69856	182	136	92	140	122	107	96	140*	68
70435	175	135	91	137*	117	106*	95*	140*	71
70425	177	142	89	152	117	100	93	139	69
70456	174	138	96	142	120	117	98	147	74
70486	-	-	85	-	-	-	-	-	-
70469	-	-	-	-	-	-	-	142	-
N	13	12	14	11	11	13	13	13	12
Mean	181.3	136.7	92.1	138.3	117.5	107.2	99.0	140.9	71.6
S.D.	5.85	4.03	3.61	5.80	3.62	5.46	4.47	3.86	3.80
FEMALES									
70461	188	132	92	131	117	98*	-	-	-
70471	180	136*	-	130	113*	92	97*	124*	-
69860	172	135	90	128	112	96	-	128*	-
70432	173	132	86	126*	107	97*	97*	130*	-
890	180	140	97	128	125	95	91	-	65
N	5	5	4	5	5	5	3	3	1
Mean	178.6	135.0	91.3	128.6	114.8	95.6	95.0	127.3	65.0
S D.	6.47	3.32	4.57	1.95	6.72	2.30	3.46	3.06	-

TABLE G1: (Continued)

Cat. No.	NH	NW	OH	OW	AL	AW	BPW	BAW	ML
MALES									
69857	49	26	33	44	56	64	118	113	181
70421	55	28	38	44	56	66*	125*	111*	182*
70430	54	23	38	39	52	62	117*	107*	173
70436	-	-	-	-	52*	-	120	113	182
70483	-	-	-	45*	56	66	129	111	175
70482	-	-	-	42*	51	66	122	114	191*
70460	60	27*	39	45	-	62	126*	112*	178*
70422	55	28	40	41	50	62	116	101	184
69861	55	24	37	41	47	65	-	98	182
69856	52	25	36	43	51	64*	123	107	180
70435	56	28	39	45	48	62	119	109	174
70425	54	29	34	41	54	65	126	115	175
70456	53	26	36	43	50	63	123	103	173
70486	-	29	-	-	-	68	121	101	-
70469	-	-	-	-	-	59	119	115	-
N	10	11	10	12	12	14	14	15	13
Mean	54.3	26.6	37.0	42.8	51.9	63.9	121.7	108.7	179.2
S.D.	2.83	2.01	2.26	1.96	3.06	2.35	3.83	5.59	5.25
FEMALES									
70461	-	-	-	-	-	-	-	112	-
70471	-	-	-	41*	51	51	108	102	179
69860	-	-	-	42*	-	63*	114	103	171
70432	-	28	-	42*	51	61	117	103	171
890	49	24	35	41	49	63	-	-	-
N	1	2	1	4	3	4	3	4	3
Mean	49.0	26.0	35.0	41.5	50.3	59.5	113.0	105.0	173.7
S.D.	-	2.83	-	0.58	1.16	5.75	4.58	4.69	4.62

TABLE G1: (Continued)

Cat. No.	LSL	RSL	SH	BL	BGW	BCW	RH	RW
MALES								
69857	87	88	38	94	100	116	69	40
70421	-	-	-	-	-	-	-	-
70430	74	80	-	-	-	-	-	-
70436	81	81	-	-	-	-	-	-
70483	77	76	40	103	113	135*	72	42
70482	90	94	35	95	109	133	62	35
70460	85*	86	33	99	99	120	65	35
70422	81	79	32	94	102*	122*	58	37
69861	78	76	37	96	-	-	-	38
69856	82	81	33	93	101	124*	59	34
70435	81	79	31	97	104*	125*	67	34
70425	86	87	32	93	116	125	59	39
70456	85	82	38	107	109*	133*	74	39
	-	-	37	97	-	-	-	-
70473	-	-	-	98	-	-	66	38
70486	74	73	38	101	108	135	54	35
70469	85	82	-	-	-	-	-	-
N	14	14	12	13	10	10	11	12
Mean	81.9	81.7	35.3	97.5	106.1	126.8	64.1	37.2
S.D.	4.83	5.53	3.03	4.18	5.78	6.76	6.27	2.59
FEMALES								
70461	82	84	-	-	-	-	-	-
70471	85	86	-	-	-	-	-	-
69860	78	80	-	-	-	-	-	-
70432	78	75	30	86	88	113	59	31
890	-	-	-	-	-	-	-	-
70450	-	-	33	91	-	-	-	-
70475	-	-	35	90	-	-	59	35
70497	-	-	34	92	93	117	61	-
70495	-	-	32	85	91	121	46	32
70421	-	-	33	88	-	-	-	-
70420	-	-	39	94	114	-	61	33
N	4	4	7	7	4	3	5	4
Mean	80.8	81.3	33.7	89.4	96.5	117.0	57.2	32.8
S.D	3.40	4 86	2.81	3.26	1.19	4.00	6.34	1.71

TABLE G2

BUSSINGER POST-CRANIAL MEASUREMENTS

Cat. No.	HL	HHD	HA-P	HM-L	RL	UL	CL	FL	FBL
MALES									
69857	-	46*	21*	21*	-	-	156*	453	450
69856	-	45*	21*	21*	-	-	147*	437	433
70435	-	51*	19	21	-	-	-	-	-
70425	-	44*	21	21	-	-	-	-	-
70456	340	47	26	27	245*	295	169	477	473
70473	327	44	22	20	256	274*	-	-	-
70486	345	44	20	21	-	-	163*	460	455
8 77	333	44	23	24	245*	264	-	464	461
70478	339	47	21	22	-	-	-	474	467
N	5	9	9	9	3	3	4	6	6
Mean	336.8	45.8	21.6	22.0	248.7	277.7	158.7	460.8	456.5
S.D.	6.94	2.33	2.01	2.18	6.35	15.82	9.47	14.66	14.14
FEMALES									
70450	292	37	18	18	-	-	-	-	-
70475	306	42	17	22	-	253	-	-	-
70496	313	40	18	21	-	-	-	-	-
70446	-	-	-	-	-	-	-	449	446
70432	272	37	18	18	-	-	-	-	-
N	4	4	4	4	-	1	-	1	1
Mean	295.7	39.0	17.8	19.8	-	253.0	-	449.0	446.0
S.D.	18.08	2.45	0.50	2.06	-	-	-	-	-

TABLE G2: (Continued)

Cat. No.	FHD	FA'-P'	FM'-L'	FA-P	FM-L	TL	TL'	TA-P	TM-L
MALES									
69857	47	31	33	29	30	380	374	37	23
69856	46	31*	29*	29	26	356	350	33	22
70435	52	33	28	32	26	-	-	37	22
70425	45	29	23	29	24	-	-	34*	22*
70456	46	32	33	33	28	393	386	38	25
70473	44	30*	-	-	-	-	-	-	-
70486	45	28	32	27	28	399	395	37	21
8 77	45	34	31	32	28	-	-	37	26
70478	48	35	33	27	28	-	-	35	25
N	9	9	8	8	8	4	4	8	8
Mean	46.4	31.4	30.3	29.8	27.3	382.0	376.3	36.0	23.3
S.D.	2.40	2.30	3.50	2.32	1.83	19.06	19.50	1.77	1.83
FEMALES									
70450	-	30	27	26	27	-	-	-	-
70475	-	-	-	-	-	-	-	-	-
70496	41	30	25	26	25	370	366	31	22
70446	-	28	24	27	22	-	-	-	-
70432	-	26	23	25	20	-	-	28	19
N	1	4	4	4	4	1	1	2	2
Mean	41.0	28.5	24.8	26.0	23.5	370.0	366.0	29.5	20.5
S.D.	-	1.92	1.71	0.82	3.11	-	-	2.12	2.12

TABLE G3

BUSSINGER MALE CRANIAL INDICES

Cat. No.	L/B	H/L	H/B	MF/B	BZ/B	L+B+H/3	OH/OW	NW/NH	NA/BZ	BP/BN	MF/BZ
69857	72.3	71.2	98.5	66.9	103.0	149.3	75.0	53.1	50.4	105.8	65.0
70421	75.7	75.1	99.3	67.1	102.1	154.7	86.4	50.9	52.4	93.5	65.7
70430	73.3	79.0	107.8	69.8	105.4	148.0	97.4	42.6	47.8	95.1	66.2
70436	75.5	74.5	98.6	68.3	102.2	153.3	-	-	-	87.2	66.9
70483	79.0	78.4	99.3	71.2	106.5	151.0	-	-	47.3	93.3	66.9
70482	70.3	-	-	66.4	100.0	-	-	-	54.0	100.0	66.4
70460	78.3	-	-	68.1	102.1	-	86.7	45.0	54.2	93.5	66.7
70422	70.4	73.1	103.8	69.5	104.6	151.0	97.6	50.9	55.5	84.2	66.4
69861	-	71.0	-	-	-	-	90.2	43.6	-	94.2	-
69856	74.7	76.9	102.9	67.6	102.9	152.7	83.7	48.1	48.6	89.7	65.7
70435	77.1	78.3	101.5	67.4	103.7	149.0	86.7	50.0	50.7	89.6	65.0
70425	80.2	85.9	107.0	62.7	97.9	157.0	82.9	53.7	49.6	93.0	64.0
70456	79.3	81.6	102.9	69.6	106.5	151.3	83.7	49.1	50.3	83.8	65.3
N	12	11	10	12	12	10	10	10	11	13	12
Mean	75.5	76.8	102.2	67.9	103.1	151.7	87.0	48.7	51.0	92.5	65.9
S.D.	3.41	4.50	3.37	2.16	2.53	2.76	6.78	3.85	2.72	6.02	0.90

TABLE H1

JUNTUNEN CRANIAL MEASUREMENTS

Cat. No.	L	B	MF	H	AH	B-N	B-P	BZ	NA
MALES									
64528	170	134*	90	133*	112	102*	96*	136*	73
64537	184	140	98	139*	120	107*	102*	152	68
64532	185*	142	97	140	121	112	110	147	81
64519	198	145*	102	147	132	113	108*	147*	79
64518	184	132*	98	127	116	102	104	132	70
41241	177	132*	91	124	109	102	99	135	67
41260	-	150*	106	-	-	111*	-	153*	78
41251	180	138	95	133	116	103*	101*	136*	67
41240	187	134*	99	143	125	99	97	136	77
41239	192	141	108	138	123	110*	105*	147*	73*
41244	197	152	102	139	124	110	108	151	79
N	10	11	11	10	10	11	10	11	11
Mean	185.4	140.0	98.7	136.3	119.8	106.5	103.0	142.9	73.8
S.D.	8.70	6.91	5.61	7.07	6.76	4.97	4.83	7.91	5.25
FEMALES									
41245	181	137	94	129	112	95	93	132	65
63177	180	140	94	134	117	99*	-	133*	-
41261	-	133*	88	-	-	-	-	-	-
64531	177	129	94	-	-	-	-	126*	-
64536	181	133*	87	-	-	-	-	-	70
64534	-	139*	99	-	-	-	102*	137*	63
63176	187	141	102	130	116	106	-	133*	-
63175	179	137	89	131	113	102	-	133	68*
41243	-	133*	84	125	111	91	94	122	65
41242	167	141	88	128	114	97	98	131	69
64535	172	-	-	-	-	-	-	-	-
N	8	10	10	6	6	6	4	8	6
Mean	178.0	136.3	91.9	129.5	113.6	98.3	96.8	130.9	66.7
S.D.	6.12	4.11	5.69	3.02	2.32	5.28	4.11	4.70	2.73

TABLE H1: (Continued)

Cat. No.	NH	NW	OH	OW	AL	AW	BPW	BAW	ML
MALES									
64528	57	24	36	42	52	64	119	108	168
64537	52	27	37	46	54*	64	130	111	183
64532	55	27	37	47	59	71	125	113	182*
64519	53	27	37	43	55*	65	130	125	196
64518	50	27*	36	41	55*	63	120	111	183
41241	52	27	34	42	51	64	117	114	175
41260	58	27	40	46	52	67	135	121	-
41251	50	27	34	43	54	65	118	118	176
41240	53	26	34	43	52	67*	120	117	185
41239	56*	26*	42	46*	55*	66	125	113	190
41244	55	24	36	46	58	65	132	118	194
N	11	11	11	11	11	11	11	11	10
Mean	53.7	26.3	36.6	44.1	54.3	65.6	124.6	115.4	183.2
S.D.	2.69	1.19	2.50	2.12	2.53	2.21	6.30	4.97	8.70
FEMALES									
41245	50	26	34	43	50	64	118	107	179
63177	-	-	-	43*	-	64*	121	107	178
41261	-	-	-	-	-	-	-	105*	-
64531	-	-	-	41*	-	62*	111	106	177
64536	51*	-	-	-	-	66	-	104*	179
64534	49	25	36	43	56	64	126	112*	-
63176	-	-	-	43*	-	64*	121	113	186
63175	52	25	33	43	-	65	122	106*	179
41243	45	25	30	39	53	64	111	103	-
41242	50	24	33	42	52*	64*	117	106	166
64535	-	-	-	-	-	60	-	-	172
N	6	5	5	8	4	10	8	10	8
Mean	49.5	25.0	33.2	42.1	52.8	63.7	118.4	106.9	177.0
S.D.	2.43	0.71	2.17	1.46	2.50	1.64	5.29	3.21	5.86

TABLE H1: (Continued)

Cat. No.	LSL	RSL	SH	BL	BGW	BCW	RH	RW
MALES								
64528	82	75	-	-	-	-	-	-
64537	89	86	34	102	107*	130	-	40
64532	80	80	42	88	109	121	65	38
64519	89	93	40	105	109	139	72	40
64518	88	90	35*	95	101	125	58	36
41241	76	88	31	84	109	124	62	33
41260	-	-	38	96	114	134	77	37
41251	82	87	32	93	101	115	59	37
41240	93	95	35	95	104	118	55	31
41239	-	-	35	100	110	123	68	35
41244	92	92	35	98	114	136	71	44
63177	-	-	37	98	92	127	55	34
64533	-	-	28	99	-	-	60	34
41250	-	-	37	98	105	135	64	34
N	9	9	13	13	12	12	12	13
Mean	85.7	87.3	35.3	96.2	106.2	127.2	63.8	36.4
S.D.	5.85	6.40	3.71	5.57	6.20	7.61	7.02	3.50
FEMALES								
41245	81	83	-	-	-	-	-	-
63177	81	80	-	-	-	-	-	-
41261	-	-	-	-	-	-	-	-
64531	83	83	-	-	-	-	-	-
64536	-	-	36	99	109	114	65	36
64534	-	-	33	93	97	115	-	32
63176	88	90	38	94	105	130	64	36
63175	81*	83	34	99	-	-	57	40
41243	80	77	34	77	87	110	47	29
41242	84	78	35	84	91	118	59	31
64535	-	-	30	95	97	116	50	32
41256	-	-	33	91	104	123	57	33
41262	-	-	36	96	103	124	59	37
N	7	7	9	9	8	8	8	9
Mean	82.6	82.0	34.3	92.0	99.1	118.7	57.3	34.0
S.D.	2.76	4.32	2.29	7.23	7.49	6.48	6.21	3.46

TABLE H2

JUNTUNEN POST-CRANIAL MEASUREMENTS

Cat. No.	HL	HHD	HA-P	HM-L	RL	UL	CL	FL	FBL
MALES									
41244	340	47	27	27	269	287	158	470	467
41240	331	43	21	22	265	281	160	476	473
41262	311	45	23	23	242	263	147*	427	424
41267	370	51	25	24	283	307	-	-	-
41264	326*	-	21*	-	256	274*	158*	-	-
41268	331	45	24	22	238*	257	157*	472	471
63180	332	46	21	24	-	-	160*	442	436
64524	352	45	22	21	-	-	-	-	-
64533	-	40*	20*	18*	-	-	156*	446	440
41250	374	50	27	25	289	313	175*	524	521
64537	294	40	24	25	-	-	155*	427	424
64532	341*	46*	22	26	270	296	161	450	447
64519	363	51	27	28	294*	310	172*	-	-
41260	339	48	24	25	273	293	166*	472	468
41251	331	43	21	24	262	281	144*	-	-
41241	321	48	21	22	242	264	155*	428	423
41239	342	45	24	24	264	291	-	462	459
64518	322	43	20	21	235	256	-	445	440
N	17	17	18	17	14	14	14	13	13
Mean	336.5	45.7	23.0	23.6	263.0	283.8	158.9	457.0	453.3
S.D.	20.41	3.32	2.38	2.45	18.75	19.22	8.30	26.89	27.46
FEMALES									
63176	320	45	20	24	247	273	154	426	421
63175	315	41	18	20	238	266	144	444	437
41243	290	37	17	16	224	244	142	415	410
41242	281	37	19	18	223	241	144	411	407
41245	320	42	23	21	258	276	-	462	460
63177	292	41	-	-	-	246	-	415	409
41261	323	41	20	19	246	-	-	446	441
41256	303	38	20	19	233	246	-	423	417
41263	-	39	-	-	-	-	-	437	430
64536	-	-	-	-	-	-	-	-	-
64535	-	39	20	18	-	-	-	-	-
64534	310	42	20	19	-	-	-	-	-
N	9	11	9	9	7	7	4	9	9
Mean	306.0	40.2	19.7	19.3	238.4	256.0	146.0	431.0	425.8
S.D.	15.26	2.44	1.66	2.24	12.84	15.04	5.42	17.29	17.78

TABLE H2: (Continued)

Cat. No.	FHD	FA'-P'	FM'-L'	FA-P	FM-L	TL	TL'	TA-P	TM-L
MALES									
41244	49	35	34	35	30	401	393	41	27
41240	45	35	29	27	27	398	390	35	26
41262	43	33	28	29	26	362	351	34	23
41267	50*	34*	-	-	-	-	-	-	-
41264	-	34	29	29*	26*	389	381	35	25
41268	49	33	27	31	28	384	379	37	22
63180	46	31	30	28	29	391	386	38	33
64524	45	29	32	-	28*	-	-	-	-
64533	40	32	29	25	25	379	374	32	22
41250	52	34	34	34	30	437	429	39	28
64537	42	33	27	29	28	378	372	36	22
64532	47	31	32	28	30	378	372	35*	25*
64519	50*	34*	-	36*	-	429	420	44	30
41260	50	33	31	32	27	406	403	39	26
41251	46	30	28	30	26	347*	342	34	21
41241	49	31	33	29	28	360	355	34	24
41239	57	34	32	31	27	383	377	33	30
64518	46	30	29	26	25	-	-	-	-
N	17	18	16	16	16	14	14	15	15
Mean	47.1	32.6	30.3	29.9	27.5	388.9	382.3	36.4	25.6
S.D.	3.36	1.82	2.35	3.11	1.67	24.87	24.47	3.27	3.50
FEMALES									
63176	47	30	31	29	29	360	354	35	24
63175	43	30	26	25	24	373	368	30	20
41243	38	30	28	25	24	351	347	29	22
41242	39	31	26	25	23	350	344	31	20
41245	45	31	30	30	28	385	380	36	25
63177	42	32	29	29	26	345	341	34	27
41261	43	32	28	28	26	358	351	31	22
41256	40	28	25	25	24	366	361	33	22
41263	44	30	28	30	25	368	362	33	24
64536	44	35	29	28	28	377	370	34	23
64535	43	29	27	-	-	-	-	-	-
64534	-	-	-	33	30	-	-	-	-
N	11	11	11	11	11	10	10	10	10
Mean	42.6	30.7	27.9	27.9	26.1	363.3	356.8	32.6	22.9
S.D.	2.66	1.85	1.81	2.66	2.34	12.84	12.69	2.27	2.18

TABLE H3

JUNTUNEN MALE CRANIAL INDICES

Cat. No.	L/B	H/L	H/B	MF/B	BZ/B	L+B+H/3	OH/OW	NW/NH	NA/BZ	BP/BN	MF/BZ
64528	78.8	78.2	99.3	67.2	101.5	145.7	85.7	42.1	53.7	94.1	66.2
64537	76.1	75.5	99.3	70.0	108.6	154.3	80.4	51.9	44.7	95.3	64.5
64532	76.8	75.7	98.6	68.3	103.5	155.7	78.7	49.1	55.1	98.2	66.0
64519	73.2	74.2	101.4	70.3	101.4	163.3	86.0	50.9	53.7	95.6	69.4
64518	71.7	69.0	96.2	74.2	100.0	147.7	87.8	54.0	53.0	102.0	74.2
41241	74.6	70.1	93.9	68.9	102.3	144.3	81.0	51.9	49.6	97.1	67.4
41260	-	-	-	70.7	102.0	-	87.0	46.6	51.0	-	-
41251	76.7	73.9	96.4	68.8	98.6	150.3	79.1	54.0	49.3	98.1	69.9
41240	71.7	76.5	106.7	73.9	101.5	154.7	79.1	49.1	56.6	98.0	72.8
41239	73.4	71.9	97.9	76.6	104.3	157.0	91.3	46.4	49.7	95.5	73.5
41244	77.2	70.6	91.4	67.1	99.3	162.7	78.3	43.6	52.3	98.2	67.5
N	10	10	10	11	11	10	11	11	11	10	10
Mean	75.0	73.6	98.1	70.6	102.1	153.6	83.1	49.1	51.7	97.2	69.1
S.D.	2.46	3.04	4.18	3.09	2.74	6.58	4.54	4.00	3.31	2.24	3.41

TABLE I1

YOUNGE CRANIAL MEASUREMENTS

Cat. No.	L	B	MF	H	AH	B-N	B-P	BZ	NA
MALES									
5011	177	140	94	126	114	105	103	140	73
5020	175	134	93	139	124	93	98*	139*	-
5068	182	149	100	138	123	106	94	142*	71
5180	-	140	95	128	114	105*	-	141*	-
5023	184	136	98	132	121	100	102*	144*	72*
5024	180	140	95	137	121	104	93	150	73*
4984	178	147	97	143	124	112	99*	149*	71*
4967	189	151	103	142	123*	113	104*	155*	-
4957	182	144	102	132	116	100	101*	147*	74*
5181	184	130	89	131	114	103	103	138	77
5001	189	147	95	137	120	111	109	144	70
4999	188	144	101	143	121	110	106	145	73
4966	188	139	100	142	121	112	100	150	72
4954	-	-	-	-	-	-	-	-	-
4996	-	143	-	135	120	-	-	-	-
4701	-	-	-	-	-	-	-	-	-
N	12	14	13	14	14	13	12	13	10
Mean	183.0	141.7	97.1	136.1	119.7	105.7	101.0	144.9	72.6
S.D.	4.86	5.90	4.05	5.60	3.69	5.89	4.61	5.06	1.96
FEMALES									
5008	-	138	-	127	111	97*	-	130*	-
4962	-	-	-	-	-	-	-	-	65*
5179	171	134	95	130	115	93	-	129*	-
4964	189	130	91	135	119	105	95	131*	69
5010	188	-	-	132	115*	100	-	-	-
4885	-	133*	-	-	-	-	-	132*	-
5022	182	135	91	129	117	103	96	133	63
5009	176	123	86	127	110*	103	103	128	68
5007	171	129*	-	137	119	99	94	128*	58
4958	176	140	95	134	118	100	-	132*	-
4997	182	136	93	131	115	99	101	129	64
N	8	9	6	9	9	9	5	9	6
Mean	179.4	133.1	91.8	131.3	115.4	99.9	97.8	130.2	64.5
S.D.	7.01	5.16	3.37	3.50	3.25	3.59	3.96	1.86	3.94

TABLE I1: (Continued)

Cat. No.	NH	NW	OH	OW	AL	AW	BPW	BAW	ML
MALES									
5011	52	24	33	44	54	65	121	107	174
5020	-	27*	-	43*	55*	-	122	111	172
5068	57	25	37	43	50*	61	121	115	179
5180	-	27*	-	43*	-	-	121	110	-
5023	-	27*	-	45*	55*	-	121	112	182
5024	52	31	34	46	50	66	126	113	176
4984	-	27*	-	45*	51*	-	132	115	176
4967	-	28*	-	47*	54*	-	134	116	186
4957	-	28*	-	46*	55*	66*	124	113	178
5181	54	30	34	42	52	69	120	107	181
5001	50	29	34	43	56	64	127	113	184
4999	56	30	36	45	53	65	124	107	185
4966	52	32	34	46	50	66	130	111	185
4954	-	-	-	-	-	-	127	111	-
4996	-	-	-	-	-	-	123	114	-
4701	-	-	-	-	-	-	133	113	-
N	7	13	7	13	12	8	16	16	12
Mean	53.3	28.1	34.6	44.5	52.9	65.3	125.4	111.7	179.8
S.D.	2.50	2.29	1.40	1.56	2.23	2.25	4.69	2.86	4.71
FEMALES									
5008	-	-	-	42*	-	63*	116	108	-
4962	48	24	33	41	-	60	-	-	-
5179	-	-	-	42*	-	63*	115	103	169
4964	49	-	33	43	51*	64*	118	107*	185
5010	-	-	-	-	-	58	-	-	187
4885	-	-	-	42*	-	64*	119	104	-
5022	50	27	32	42	47	65*	116	107	180
5009	49	28	34	38	55*	65*	116*	100*	175
5007	43	25	31	41	49	63*	114	97	168
4958	-	27	-	42*	-	65*	119	113	172
4997	48	25	33	42	54	65	120	109	179
N	6	6	6	10	5	11	9	9	8
Mean	47.8	26.0	32.7	41.5	51.2	63.2	117.0	105.3	176.9
S.D.	2.48	1.55	1.03	1.35	3.35	2.27	2.06	4.87	7.08

TABLE I1: (Continued)

Cat. No.	LSL	RSL	SH	BL	BGW	BCW	RH	RW
MALES								
5011	79	76	-	-	-	-	-	-
5020	84	84	-	-	-	-	-	-
5068	79	85	-	-	-	-	-	-
5180	86	84	-	-	-	-	-	-
5023	86	87	36*	95	109	130*	60	32
5024	85	88	36*	105	115*	136*	68	35*
4984	-	-	35	99	110	128	69	38
4967	86	92	-	95	117	149	72	-
4957	79	80	-	92	103	131*	-	-
5181	80	80	-	-	-	-	-	-
5001	79	75	35*	98	114	131	67	38*
4999	81	81	37	102	103	129*	65	39
4966	80	81	36	101	117	137*	63	34
5002	-	-	32	87	99	116	64	31
4996	-	-	-	99	108	130	67	30
4954	87	85	36	83	-	-	73	32
4996	-	-	-	-	-	-	-	-
4701	84	78	-	-	-	-	-	-
N	14	14	8	11	10	10	10	9
Mean	82.5	82.6	35.4	96.0	109.5	131.7	66.8	34.3
S.D.	3.18	4.75	1.51	6.57	6.33	8.30	3.99	3.35
FEMALES								
5008	80	82	-	89	97	-	57	-
4692	-	-	-	-	-	-	-	-
5179	84	85	-	-	-	-	-	-
4964	84	84	-	-	-	-	-	-
5010	83*	86	-	-	-	-	-	-
4885	78	76	-	-	-	-	-	-
5022	78	83	-	-	-	-	-	-
5009	79	80*	-	-	-	-	-	-
5007	75	78	-	-	-	-	-	-
4958	76	83	-	-	-	-	-	-
4997	85	87	33	97	101	121	55	32
4962	-	-	33	85	-	-	57	33
4968	-	-	34	91	116	126	64	33
N	10	10	3	4	3	2	4	3
Mean	80.2	82.4	33.3	90.5	104.7	123.5	58.3	32.7
S.D.	3.58	3.50	0.58	5.00	10.02	3.54	3.95	0.58

TABLE I3

YOUNGE MALE CRANIAL INDICES

Cat. No.	L/B	H/L	H/B	MF/B	BZ/B	L+B+H/3	OH/OW	NW/NH	NA/BZ	BP/BN	MF/BZ
5011	79.1	71.2	90.0	67.1	100.0	152.3	75.0	46.2	52.1	98.1	67.1
5020	76.6	79.4	103.7	69.4	103.7	149.3	-	-	-	105.4	66.9
5068	81.9	75.8	92.6	67.1	95.3	156.3	86.0	43.9	50.0	88.7	70.4
5180	-	-	91.4	67.9	100.7	-	-	-	-	-	67.4
5023	73.9	71.7	97.1	72.1	105.9	154.7	-	-	50.0	102.0	68.1
5024	77.8	76.1	97.9	67.9	107.1	152.3	73.9	59.6	48.7	98.4	63.5
4984	82.6	80.3	97.3	66.0	101.4	156.0	-	-	47.7	88.4	65.1
4967	79.9	75.1	94.0	68.2	102.6	160.7	-	-	-	92.0	66.5
4957	79.1	72.5	91.7	70.8	102.1	152.7	-	-	50.3	101.0	69.4
5181	70.7	71.2	100.8	68.5	106.2	148.3	81.0	55.6	55.8	100.0	64.5
5001	77.8	72.5	93.2	64.6	98.0	157.7	79.1	58.0	48.6	98.2	66.0
4999	76.6	76.1	99.3	70.1	100.7	158.3	80.1	53.6	50.3	96.4	69.7
4966	73.9	75.5	102.2	71.9	107.9	156.3	73.9	61.5	48.0	89.3	66.7
N	12	12	13	13	13	12	7	7	10	12	13
Mean	77.5	74.8	96.3	68.6	102.4	154.6	78.4	54.1	50.2	96.5	67.0
S.D.	3.44	3.05	4.44	2.22	3.69	3.69	4.47	6.70	2.38	5.58	2.03

TABLE J1

BACKLUND CRANIAL MEASUREMENTS

Cat. No.	L	B	MF	H	AH	B-N	B-P	BZ	NA
MALES									
455483	181	143*	100	-	-	107*	101*	145*	69*
455481	186	158	98	134	118	105	101	156	74
455488	188	159	106	145	124	107	95	152	73
455482	181	148	99	135	119	102	95	151	76
4554810	187	153	95	130	119	110	108	153	75
N	5	5	5	4	4	5	5	5	5
Mean	184.6	152.2	99.6	136.0	120.0	106.2	100.0	151.4	73.4
S.D.	3.36	6.76	4.04	6.38	2.71	2.95	5.39	4.04	2.70
FEMALES									
62669	171	144	91	130	112	101	93	132	67
455485	171	140	-	118	107	94	88	122	59

Cat No.	NH	NW	OH	OW	AL	AW	BPW	BAW	ML
MALES									
455483	-	28*	-	44*	53*	-	128	115	179
455481	49	28	34	40	58	68	144	124	185
455488	54	30	36	44	49	65	136	116	184
455482	49	26	37	41	54	61	131	112	179
4554810	56	27	37	46	58	66	131	114	185
N	4	5	4	5	5	4	5	6	5
Mean	52.0	27.8	36.0	43.0	54.4	65.0	134.0	116.2	182.4
S.D.	3.56	1.48	1.41	2.45	3.78	2.94	6.29	4.60	3.13
FEMALES									
62669	51	33	36	42	50*	61	122	112	171
455485	42	25	33	41	47*	56	117	111	171

Cat. No.	LSL	RSL	SH	BL	BGW	BCW	RH	RW
MALES								
455483	78	78	32	97	110	143	50	34
455481	89	91	34	99	108	142	65	37
455488	87	85	36*	93	105	135	71	32
455482	84	84	32	112	112*	137*	-	37*
4554810	84	84	-	-	-	-	-	-
455486	-	-	37	-	-	-	-	41
455489	-	-	34	93	107	-	68	33
N	5	5	6	5	5	4	4	6
Mean	84.4	84.4	34.2	98.8	108.4	139.2	63.5	35.7
S.D.	4.16	4.62	2.04	7.82	2.70	3.86	9.33	3.33
FEMALES								
62669	76	83	32	95	100	-	60	31
455485	85	84	-	-	-	-	-	-
4554811	-	-	34	109	-	-	63	40

TABLE J2

BACKLUND POST-CRANIAL MEASUREMENTS

Cat. No.	HL	HHD	HA-P	HM-L	RL	UL	CL	FL	FBL
MALES									
455482	339	47	22	24	-	-	152*	-	-
455483	339*	48*	22*	22*	268	292	-	446	443
455481	333	51	22	22	262	280*	158	-	-
455484	338	52	22	24	267	284	160	476	473
455487	355*	50	24	19	282	301	-	496	492
4554810	340	50	21	23	264	281	-	453	448
N	6	6	6	6	5	5	3	4	4
Mean	340.7	49.7	22.2	22.3	268.6	287.6	156.7	467.7	464.0
S.D.	7.45	1.86	0.98	1.86	7.86	8.85	4.16	22.78	22.82
FEMALE									
45548	275	39	22	18	228	-	-	419	411

Cat. No.	FHD	FA'-P'	FM'-L'	FA-P	FM-L	TL	TL'	TA-P	TM-L
MALES									
455482	47	28	34	29	29	383	364	36	21
455483	49	26	35	31	28	-	-	37*	19*
455481	50*	34*	-	-	-	-	-	-	-
455484	53	27	37	32	30	394	387	40	22
455487	50	30	39	34	29	-	-	41	26
4554810	49	29	25	29	28	-	-	38	21
N	6	6	5	5	5	2	2	5	5
Mean	49.7	29.0	34.0	31.0	28.8	388.5	375.5	38.4	21.8
S.D.	1.97	2.83	5.39	2.12	0.84	7.78	16.26	2.07	2.59
FEMALE									
45548	45	26	26	26	24	-	-	-	-

TABLE J3

BACKLUND MALE CRANIAL INDICES

Cat. No.	L/B	H/L	H/B	MF/B	BZ/B	L+B+H/3	OH/OW	NW/NH	NA/BZ	BP/BN	MF/BZ
455483	79.0	-	-	69.4	101.4	-	-	-	47.6	94.4	69.0
455481	84.9	72.0	84.8	62.0	98.7	159.3	85.0	57.1	47.4	96.2	68.2
455488	84.6	77.1	9.12	66.7	95.6	164.0	81.8	55.6	48.0	88.8	69.7
455482	81.8	74.6	91.2	66.9	102.0	154.7	90.2	53.1	50.3	93.1	65.6
4554810	81.8	69.5	85.0	62.1	100.0	156.7	80.4	48.2	49.0	98.2	62.1
N	5	4	4	5	5	4	4	4	5	5	5
Mean	82.4	73.3	88.1	65.4	99.5	158.7	84.4	53.5	48.5	94.1	66.9
S.D.	2.42	3.28	3.64	3.26	2.55	4.02	4.35	3.90	1.20	3.55	3.11

BIBLIOGRAPHY

Adis-Castro, E. and G. K. Neumann
1948 The Incidence of Ear Exostoses in the Hopewell People of the Illinois Valley. Proceedings of the Indiana Academy of Science Vol. 57:33-36.

Allbrook, D. B.
1956 Changes in Lumbar Vertebral Body Height with Age. American Journal of Physical Anthropology Vol. 14:35-40.

Anderson, J. E.
1968 The Serpent Mounds Site Physical Anthropology. Occasional Paper No. 11, Art and Archaeology. Royal Ontario Museum, University of Toronto.

Baer, M. J.
1956 Dimensional Changes in the Human Head and Face in the Third Decade of Life. American Journal of Physical Anthropology Vol. 14:557-75.

Barry, R. J.
1968 The Biology of Non-metrical Variation in Mice and Men. *In*: D. R. Brothwell (ed.), The Skeletal Biology of Earlier Human Populations, pp. 103-33. Pergamon Press. London.

Boas, F.
1911 Changes in Bodily Form of Descendants of Immigrants. Senate Document 208, 61st Congress, 2nd Session. Washington, D.C.

Boyne, A. W.
1960 Secular Changes in the Stature of Adults and the Growth of Children, with Special Reference to Changes in Intelligence of 11 Year-olds. *In*: J. M. Tanner (ed.), Human Growth. Pergamon Press. London.

Brace, C. L.
1962 Cultural Factors in the Evolution of the Human Dentition. *In*: M. F. A. Montagu (ed.), Culture and the Evolution of Man, pp. 343-54. Oxford University Press. New York.

Brace, C. L. and M. F. A. Montagu
1965 Man's Evolution: An Introduction to Physical Anthropology. MacMillan. New York.

Brooks, S. T.
1955 Skeletal Age at Death: The Reliability of Cranial and Pubic Indicators. American Journal of Physical Anthropology Vol. 13:567-98.

Brose, D. S.
1968 The Backlund Mound Group. Wisconsin Archeologist Vol. 49: 34-51.

Caldwell, J. R.
1964 Interaction Spheres in Prehistory. *In*: J. R. Caldwell and R. L. Hall (eds.), Hopewellian Studies, Illinois State Museum Scientific Papers Vol. 12, No. 6.

Clark, P. J.
1952 An Extension of the Coefficient of Divergence for Use with Multiple Characters. Copeia, pp. 61-64.
1956 The Heritability of Certain Anthropometric Characters as Ascertained from Measurements of Twins. American Journal of Human Genetics Vol. 8:49-54.

Crane, H. R. and J. B. Griffin
1963 University of Michigan Radiocarbon Dates, VIII. Radiocarbon Vol. 5:228-53.

De Villiers, H.
1968 The Skull of the South African Negro. Witwatersrand University Press. Johannesburg.

Dixon, W. J. (ed.)
1968 Biomedical Computer Programs. University of California Press. Berkeley.

Driver, H. E.
1965 Survey of Numerical Classifications in Anthropology. *In*: D. Hymes (ed.), The Use of Computers in Anthropology, pp. 301-44. Moulton and Company. The Hague.

Eyman, C. E.
1964 Physical Anthropology of the Juntunen Site. Unpublished paper read at the 1964 meeting of the Society for American Archaeology. Chapel Hill.
1966 The Schultz Focus: A Plains Middle Woodland Burial Complex in Eastern Kansas. M. A. thesis submitted to the Faculty of Graduate Studies. University of Calgary. Calgary.
n.d. A comparison of Michigan and other Hopewellian skeletal remains. Manuscript on file at the University of Michigan Museum of Anthropology.

Eyman, C. E. and R. L. Bettarel
1965 Physical Anthropology of the Juntunen Site, 20MK1, Bois Blanc Island, Michigan. Paper presented at the 69th Annual Meeting, Michigan Academy of Science, Arts and Letters. Ann Arbor.

Falconer, D. S.
1964 Introduction to Quantitative Genetics. Oliver and Boyd. London.

Fishberg, M.
1905 Materials for the Physical Anthropology of the Eastern European Jew. Annals of the New York Academy of Science Vol. 16:155-297.

Fitting, J. E.
1965 Late Woodland Cultures of Southeastern Michigan. Anthropological Papers, Museum of Anthropology, University of Michigan No. 24. Ann Arbor.

1966 Radiocarbon Dating the Younge Tradition. American Antiquity Vol. 31:738.

Flanders, R. E.
1965 A Comparison of Some Middle Woodland Materials from Illinois and Michigan. Unpublished Ph.D. Dissertation. University of Michigan. Ann Arbor.

Garn, S. M., A. B. Lewis and A. J. Walenga
1968 Crown-size Profile Pattern Comparisons of 14 Human Populations. Archives of Oral Biology Vol. 13:1235-42.

Garn, S. M., C. G. Rohmann and K. P. Hertzog
1969 Apparent Influence of the X Chromosome on Timing of 73 Ossification Centers. American Journal of Physical Anthropology Vol. 30:123-28.

Garn, S. M., C. G. Rohmann, B. Wagner and W. Ascoli
1967 Continuing Bone Growth Throughout Life: A General Phenomenon. American Journal of Physical Anthropology Vol. 26:313-17.

Garn, S. M., B. Wagner, C. G. Rohmann and W. Ascoli
1968 Further Evidence for Continuing Bone Expansion. American Journal of Physical Anthropology Vol. 28:219-22.

Garrett, H. E.
1958 Statistics in Psychology and Education. David McKay Company. New York.

Genoves, S.
1967 Proportionality of the Long Bones and Their Relation to Stature among Mesoamericans. American Journal of Physical Anthropology Vol. 26:67-78.

Giles, E. and O. Elliot
1963 Sex Determination by Discriminant Function Analysis of Crania. American Journal of Physical Anthropology Vol. 21:53-68.

Goldstein, M. S.
1936 Changes in Dimensions and Forms of the Face and Head with Age. American Journal of Physical Anthropology Vol. 22:37-89.

1943 Demographic and Bodily Changes in Descendants of Mexican Immigrants with Comparable Data on Parents and Children in Mexico. Institute of Latin American Studies. Austin, Texas. (Cited by Lasker, 1946.)

Greenman, E. F.
1937 The Younge Site: An Archaeological Record from Michigan. Occasional Contributions from the Museum of Anthropology of the University of Michigan No. 6. Ann Arbor.

Griffin, J. B.
1943 The Fort Ancient Aspect: Its Cultural and Chronological Position in Mississippi Valley Archaeology. Anthropological Papers, Museum of Anthropology, University of Michigan No. 28. Ann Arbor.

1946 Cultural Change and Continuity in Eastern United States Archaeology. *In*: F. Johnson (ed.), Man in Northeastern North America. Papers of the Robert S. Peabody Foundation for Archaeology Vol. 3:37-95.

1958 The Chronological Position of the Hopewellian Culture in the Eastern United States. Anthropological Papers, Museum of Anthropology, University of Michigan No. 12. Ann Arbor.

1960 Climatic Change: A Contributory Cause of the Growth and Decline of Northern Hopewellian Culture. Wisconsin Archeologist Vol. 14:21-33.

1967 Eastern North American Archaeology: A Summary. Science Vol. 156:175-91.

Gruneberg, H.

1952 Genetical Studies on the Skeleton of the Mouse. IV Quasi-continuous Variations. Journal of Genetics Vol. 51:95-114.

Halsey, J. R.

1968 The Springwells Mound Group of Wayne County, Michigan. *In*: Contributions to Michigan Archaeology, Anthropological Papers, Museum of Anthropology, University of Michigan No. 32:79-159. Ann Arbor.

Hanna, B. L.

1962 The Biological Relationships Among Indian Groups of the Southwest: Analysis of Morphological Traits. American Journal of Physical Anthropology Vol. 20:499-508.

Harrison, G. A., J. S. Weiner, J. M. Tanner and N. A. Barnicot

1964 Human Biology. An Introduction to Human Evolution, Variation and Growth. Oxford University Press. New York.

Hiernaux, J.

1963 Heredity and Environment: Their Influence on Human Morphology. A Comparison of Two Independent Lines of Study. American Journal of Physical Anthropology Vol. 21:575-90.

1968 La diversite humaine en Afrique subsaharienne. Editions de l'Institut de Sociologie, Universite Libre de Bruxelles.

Hooton, E. A.

1922 Appendix. *In*: C. C. Willoughby, The Turner Group of Earthworks, Hamilton County, Ohio. Papers of the Peabody Museum of American Archaeology and Ethnology, Harvard University Vol. VIII, No. 3.

1930 The Indians of Pecos Pueblo. Papers of the Southwestern Expedition No. 4. Yale University Press. New Haven.

Howells, W. W.

1957 The Cranial Vault: Factors in Size and Shape. American Journal of Physical Anthropology Vol. 15:19-48.

1966 The Jomon Population of Japan. A Study by Discriminant Analysis of Japanese and Ainu Crania. Papers of the Peabody Museum of Archaeology and Ethnology, Harvard University Vol. LVII:3-43. Cambridge.

Hrdlicka, A.
1906 Contribution to the Physical Anthropology of California. University of California Publications in American Archaeology and Ethnology Vol. 4:49-64.

Huber, N. M.
1968 The Problem of Stature Increase: Looking from the Past to the Present. *In*: D. R. Brothwell (ed.), The Skeletal Biology of Earlier Human Populations, pp. 67-102. Pergamon Press. London.

Hunter, K. B.
1968 Preliminary Report on the Hopewellian Skeletons from the Pete Klunk Site, Calhoun County, Illinois. Illinois Archaeological Survey Bull. 6:125-28.

Israel, H.
1967 Continuing Growth in the Human Cranial Skeleton. Archives of Oral Biology Vol. 13:133-38.

Jamison, P. L.
1969 A Demographic and Comparative Analysis of the Albany Mounds Hopewell Skeletons. Unpublished M. A. Thesis. University of Wisconsin. Madison.

Johnson, C. C., R. J. Gorlin and V. E. Anderson
1965 Torus Mandibularis: A Genetic Study. American Journal of Human Genetics Vol. 17:433-42.

Johnston, R. B.
1968 The Archaeology of the Serpent Mounds Site. Occasional Paper No. 10, Art and Archaeology, Royal Ontario Museum, University of Toronto.

Kaplan, B. A.
1954 Environment and Human Plasticity. American Anthropologist Vol. 56:780-800.

Kronfeld, R.
1935 Development and Calcification of the Human Deciduous and Permanent Dentition. The Bur Vol. 35:18-25.

Landauer, C. H.
1962 A Factor Analysis of the Facial Skeleton. Human Biology Vol. 34:239-54.

Lasker, G. L.
1946 Migration and Physical Differentiation. American Journal of Physical Anthropology Vol. 4:273-300.

Laughlin, W. S. and J. B. Jorgensen
1956 Isolate Variation in Greenlandic Eskimo Crania. Acta Genetica et Statistica Medica Vol. 6:3-12.

Long, J. K.
1966 A Test of Multiple-discriminant Analysis as a Means of Determining Evolutionary Changes and Inter-group Relations in Physical Anthropology. American Anthropologist Vol. 68: 444-64.

McCall, W. A.
1939 Measurement. MacMillan. New York.

McGregor, J. C.
1958 The Pool and Irving Villages: A Study of Hopewell Occupation in the Illinois River Valley. University of Illinois Press. Urbana.

McPherron, A.
1967 The Juntunen Site and the Late Woodland Prehistory of the Upper Great Lakes Area. Anthropological Papers, Museum of Anthropology, University of Michigan No. 30. Ann Arbor.

Mahalanobis, P. C.
1936 On the Generalized Distance in Statistics. Proceedings of the National Institute of Sciences, India Vol. 12:49-55.

Mahalanobis, P. C., D. A. Majumdar and C. R. Rao
1949 Anthropometric Survey of the United Provinces, 1941: A Statistical Study. Sankya Vol. 9:93-324.

Meredith, H. V.
1946 Order and Age of Eruption of the Deciduous Dentition. Journal of Dental Research Vol. 25:43-66.

Morse, D. F.
1963 The Steuben Village and Mounds: A Multicomponent Late Hopewell Site in Illinois. Anthropological Papers, Museum of Anthropology, University of Michigan No. 21. Ann Arbor.

Neumann, G. K.
1937 Preliminary Notes on the Crania from Fulton County. *In*: F. C. Cole and T. Deuel (eds.), Rediscovering Illinois, pp. 227-64. University of Chicago Press. Chicago.
1942 Types of Artificial Cranial Deformation in the Eastern United States. American Antiquity Vol. 7:306-10.
1952*a* Archaeology and Race in the American Indian. *In*: J. B. Griffin (ed.), Archaeology of the Eastern United States, pp. 13-34. University of Chicago Press. Chicago.
1952*b* Measurements and Indices of American Indian Varieties. Yearbook of Physical Anthropology, 1952, pp. 243-55.
1960 Origins of the Indians of the Middle Mississippian Area. Proceedings of the Indiana Academy of Science Vol. 69:66-68.

Neumann, G. K. and M. L. Fowler
1952 Hopewellian Sites in the Lower Wabash Valley. *In*: T. Deuel (ed.), Hopewellian Communities in Illinois, Illinois State Museum, Scientific Papers Vol. 5:175-248.

Osborne, R. H. and F. V. DeGeorge
1959 Genetic Basis of Morphological Variation. Harvard University Press. Cambridge.

Ostertag, W.
1959 Genetic and Environmental Factors Influencing Certain Anthropometric Traits. Proceedings of the Indiana Academy of Science Vol. 68:59-64.

Pearson, K. and A. G. Davin
1924 On the Biometric Constants of the Human Skull. Biometrika Vol. 16:328-63.

Pearson, K. and A. Lee
1903 On the Laws of Inheritance in Man. I: Inheritance of Physical Characteristics. Biometrika Vol. 2:357-462.

Perino, G. H.
1968 The Pete Klunk Mound Group, Calhoun County, Illinois. The Archaic and Hopewell Occupations. Illinois Archaeological Survey Bull. 6:9-124.

Perkins, R. W.
1965 The Frederick Site. Illinois Archaeological Survey Bull. 5: 68-94.

Phenice, T. W.
1968 The Schultz Mounds Skeletal Material: A Descriptive and Comparative Analysis. Unpublished Ph.D. Dissertation. University of Kansas.

Potzger, J. E.
1946 Phytosociology of the Primeval Forest in Central-northern Wisconsin and Upper Michigan and a Brief Post-glacial History of the Lake Forest Formation. Ecological Monographs Vol. 16:211-50.

Prufer, O. H.
1964*a* The Hopewell Cult. Scientific American Vol. 211, No. 6:90-102.
1964*b* The Hopewell Complex of Ohio. *In*: J. R. Caldwell and R. L. Hall (eds.), Hopewellian Studies, Illinois State Museum, Scientific Papers Vol. 12, No. 2.

Rao, C. R.
1952 Advanced Statistical Methods in Biometric Research. John Wiley and Sons, Inc. New York.

Ritchie, W. A.
1965 The Archaeology of New York State. Natural History Press. Garden City, N.Y.

Robbins, L. M.
1968 The Identification of the Prehistoric Shawnee Indians. The Description of the Population of the Fort Ancient Aspect. Unpublished Ph.D. Dissertation. Indiana University.

Scott, J. H.
1957 Muscle Growth and Function in Relation to Skeletal Morphology. American Journal of Physical Anthropology Vol. 15: 197-234.

Selby, S., S. M. Garn and V. Kanareff
1955 The Incidence and Familial Nature of a Bony Bridge on the First Cervical Vertebra. American Journal of Physical Anthropology Vol. 13:129-41.

Siebert, F. T., Jr.
1967 The Original Home of the Proto-Algonquian People. *In*: Contributions to Anthropology: Linguistics I. National Museum of Canada, Anthropological Series No. 78, Bull. 214: 13-59.

Snow, C. E.
1948 Indian Knoll Skeletons of Site Oh2, Ohio County, Kentucky. University of Kentucky Reports in Anthropology Vol. 4, No. 3, Pt. 2.

Stevenson, P. H.
1924 Age Order of Epiphyseal Union in Man. American Journal of Physical Anthropology Vol. 7, No. 1:53-93.

Stewart, T. D.
1940 New Evidence of the Physical Type of Bearers of the Hopewellian Culture. American Journal of Physical Anthropology Vol. 27 (O.S.), Supplement to No. 2, Pg. 15.
1943 Skeletal Remains from Platte and Clay Counties, Missouri. *In*: W. R. Wedel (ed.), Archaeological Investigations in Platte and Clay Counties, Missouri. United States National Museum, Bull. 183:245-73.

Stewart, T. D. (ed.)
1952 Hrdlicka's Practical Anthropometry. Wistar Institute of Anatomy and Biology. Philadelphia.
1962 Comments on the Reassessment of the Indian Knoll Skeletons. American Journal of Physical Anthropology Vol. 20:143-47.

Stewart, T. D. and T. W. McKern
1957 Skeletal Age Changes in Young American Males. Quartermaster Research and Development Center, Environmental Protection Division, Technical Report EP-45. Natick, Mass.

Struever, S.
1964 The Hopewell Interaction Sphere in Riverine—Western Great Lakes Culture History. *In*: J. R. Caldwell and R. L. Hall (eds.), Hopewellian Studies, Illinois State Museum, Scientific Papers Vol. 12, No. 3.

Suzuki, M. and T. Sakai
1960 A Familial Study of Torus Palatinus and Torus Mandibularis. American Journal of Physical Anthropology Vol. 18:263-72.

Tanner, J. M.
1962 Growth at Adolescence. Blackwell Scientific Publications. Oxford.
1964 Human Growth and Constitution. *In*: G. A. Harrison, J. S. Weiner, J. M. Tanner and N. A. Barnicot, Human Biology: An Introduction to Human Evolution, Variation and Growth, pp. 299-397. Oxford University Press. New York.

Tekiner, R. M.
1963 Appendix. *In*: J. A. Ford, Hopewell Culture Burial Mounds Near Helena, Arkansas. American Museum of Natural History, Anthropological Papers Vol. 50, No. 1:48-53.

Todd, T. W. and D. W. Lyon, Jr.
1924 Endocranial Suture Closure. I: Adult Males of White Stock. American Journal of Physical Anthropology Vol. 7, No. 3: 325-84.

Trotter, M. and G. C. Gleser
1958 A Re-evaluation of Estimation of Stature Based on Measurements of Stature Taken During Life and of Long Bones After Death. American Journal of Physical Anthropology Vol. 16: 79-123.

Vandenberg, S. G.
1962 How "Stable" are Hereditary Estimates? A Comparison of Heritability Estimates from Six Anthropometric Studies. American Journal of Physical Anthropology Vol. 20:331-38.

Vandenberg, S. G. and H. H. Strandskov
1964 A Comparison of Identical and Fraternal Twins on some Anthropometric Measures. Human Biology Vol. 36:45-52.

Washburn, S. L.
1947 The Relation of the Temporal Muscle to the Form of the Skull. The Anatomical Record Vol. 99:239-48.

Webb, W. S. and C. E. Snow
1945 The Adena People. University of Kentucky Reports in Anthropology Vol. 6:1-369.

Wilkinson, R. G.
1968 Skeletal Analysis of the Fort Wayne Mound. *In*: J. E. Fitting, J. R. Halsey and H. M. Wobst, Contributions to Michigan Archaeology. Anthropological Papers, Museum of Anthropology, University of Michigan, No. 32:161-71. Ann Arbor.

Wolanski, N. and J. Charzewska
1967 Similarity of some Anthropological Characteristics of Parents and Offspring in Different Phases of Ontogenetic Development. Acta Genetica et Statistica Medica, Vol. 17:365-81.

Wolpoff, M. H.
1968 Climatic Influence on the Skeletal Nasal Aperture. American Journal of Physical Anthropology Vol. 29:405-23.

Wray, D. E. and R. S. MacNeish
1961 The Hopewellian and Weaver Occupations of the Weaver Site, Fulton County, Illinois. Illinois State Museum, Scientific Papers Vol. 7, No. 2.

Young, P. D.
1960 The Frederick Site—Sc11. *In*: E. A. Bluhm (ed.), Indian Mounds and Villages in Illinois. Illinois Archaeological Survey, Bull. 2.

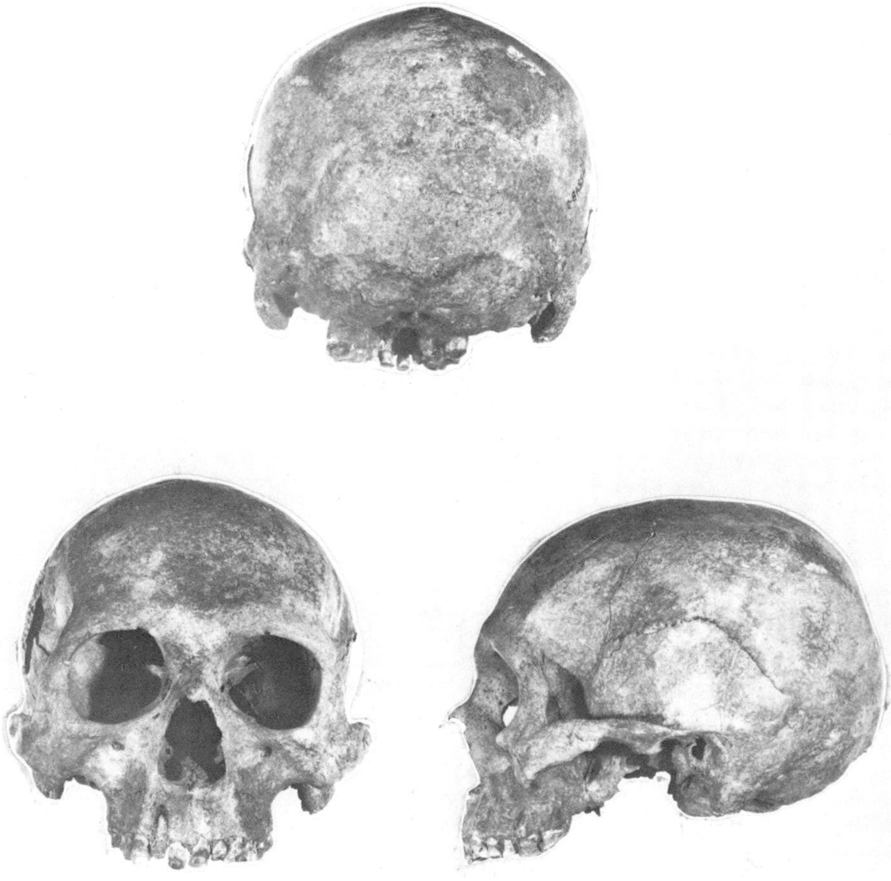

Adult Male from the Backlund Site (4554810).

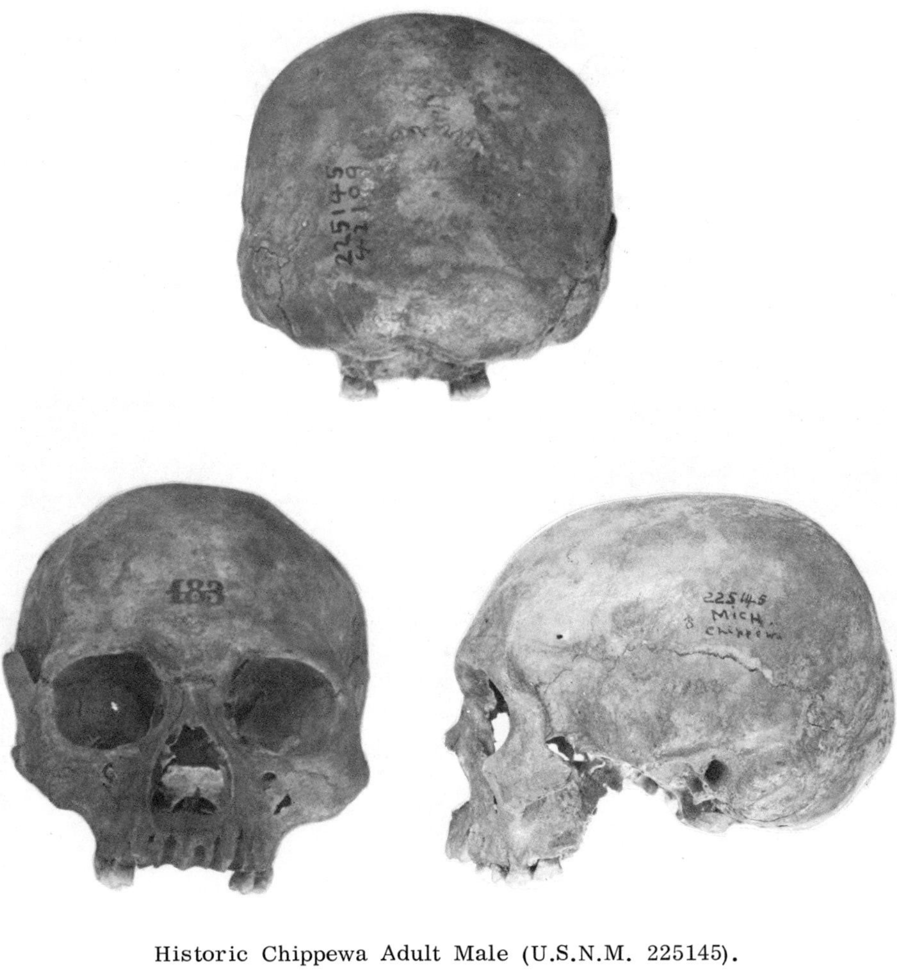

Historic Chippewa Adult Male (U.S.N.M. 225145).